NEW PERSPECTIVES ON THE SOUTH

Charles P. Roland, General Editor

Nineteenth-Century
SOUTHERN
LITERATURE

J. V. Ridgely

THE UNIVERSITY PRESS OF KENTUCKY

ISBN: 0–8131–0301–0

Library of Congress Catalog Card Number: 79–4011

Copyright © 1980 by The University Press of Kentucky

Scholarly publisher for the Commonwealth,
serving Berea College, Centre College of Kentucky,
Eastern Kentucky University, The Filson Club,
Georgetown College, Kentucky Historical Society,
Kentucky State University, Morehead State University,
Murray State University, Northern Kentucky University,
Transylvania University, University of Kentucky,
University of Louisville, and Western Kentucky University.

Editorial and Sales Offices: Lexington, Kentucky 40506

To Julia

Contents

Editor's Preface

SOUTHERN society has traditionally been an extraordinarily verbal society. Words, spoken and written, have been the region's primary means of intellectual, political, and spiritual expression. The politicians, journalists, and preachers of the Old South mobilized the language to explain and defend the region's "peculiar institution" and unusual "way of life." Especially to defend them. So did most of the poets and novelists. Only the southern humorists, a paradoxical group of writers who turned for inspiration to the antics of the poor whites, did not employ their pens as weapons in the cause of southern sectionalism. Possibly even they, consciously or not, helped to parry the thrust of the abolitionists.

Except for the verse and short stories of Edgar Allan Poe, the Old South did not produce a great imaginative literature. Mr. Ridgely demonstrates that southern men of letters almost altogether subordinated art to sectional orthodoxy. A vivid illustration of this truth is shown in the career of the Old South's most celebrated novelist, William Gilmore Simms of Charleston. As for Poe, his identity as a full southerner may be questioned. Certainly he viewed himself as more than a "southern writer."

Mr. Ridgely tells how the defeat of the Confederacy added a new tragic theme to southern poetry, and how the changed conditions of postwar life gave rise to the local-color school of southern writing. The ranks of orthodoxy were not quite so close as among the writers of the Old South. George Washington Cable of Louisiana spoke out for civil rights for the blacks; Mark Twain, born and bred a southerner, disdained his native region's prejudice and provincialism. But Cable and Twain became self-imposed exiles from the South. The most authoritative literary voice remaining in the region—that of Thomas Nelson Page of Virginia—cast a glorious mantle over its past.

In producing this able study, Mr. Ridgely calls upon an information and understanding of southern literature gained from years of teaching it and writing about it. By describing the relationship between southern imaginative literature and the broader aspects of the region's history and culture, and by showing the influence of nineteenth-century southern literature on the Southern Renascence of the twentieth century, he makes his work highly suitable for a volume of "New Perspectives on the South." The series is designed to give a fresh and comprehensive view of the South's history, as seen in the light of the striking developments since World War II in the affairs of the region. Each volume is expected to be a complete essay representing both a synthesis of the best scholarship on the subject and an interpretive analysis derived from the author's own reflections.

CHARLES P. ROLAND

PROLOG

The Southron

"OH, WHO AM I?" The words open Robert Penn Warren's novel *Band of Angels*, the tale of a southern belle who learns that she is part black, is sold into bondage, and at last achieves a selfhood out of the inherited division of her being. The theme of the quest for one's true identity is, of course, universal; self-definition is a primary need. But in American literature the problem has had a peculiar resonance. For the first English settler on the coastline was a man who was as yet without a country. Severed from close ties with a homeland, bereft of familiar and fostering institutions, awed at first—in F. Scott Fitzgerald's haunting phrase—by the "presence of this continent," the colonial struck out into the heart of the Golden Land, not comprehending that it was also a heart of darkness in which he had to lose himself before he could find a self. The material gains could soon be counted; the psychic cost of the venture into the wilderness could hardly be reckoned. It was indeed, as Henry James observed, a complex fate to be an American. For the antebellum southern American it would be a disastrous one as well.

For the question shifted emphasis in the South: not just "Who am I?" but "Who are *we?*" The variety of responses, sometimes confused, at times aggressively dogmatic, illuminates the pressures upon a people to create a comprehensive nurturing myth. To impose an order upon radical contradictions—to portray a society in which each individual would know who he was because he knew his place—would be a portion of the task of the writers to be surveyed here. But let it be emphasized at the outset that these authors by themselves could not have led hypnotized readers into

an assertion of southern selfhood. They but responded to a bur-
geoning political and social necessity; they supplied the usable
fiction. This notion of regional uniqueness began early, and we
shall first look for its roots in the primal colonial experience. Its
growth was gradual, but by the 1830s, when the slavery issue
began to dominate southern thought, local writers were fully
prepared to retell this history in the light of current needs, to assure
their readers that the path from Jamestown to the present had
been straight and unbroken. Their chief vehicle, almost inevitably,
was the historical romance. The genre, as recently formulated by
Sir Walter Scott, had, of course, swept over the whole nation; but
to southerners it had a special appeal, for it fostered nationalism
and authenticated hierarchy. It made the never-never a model
for the here-and-now.

It is said that in 1819 Thomas Jefferson's daughter Martha
persuaded her father to look into that delirious success, Scott's
Ivanhoe. Jefferson could not finish it; he found it the dullest and
driest reading he had encountered. One would not expect the
denouncer of a king to take much joy in a gaudy parade of knights
and monarchs; but Jefferson's distaste reflected an earlier rationalistic cast of mind. Why read a fiction—a self-evident lie—when
one could ponder the truth of the facts of history? His fellow
"Southrons" (the term was appropriated from Scott) would follow
a newer, romantic line. To fictionalize their pasts and to mythify
their present institutions, and to cast these imaginative constructs
with themselves in self-satisfying roles, was to be a deadly serious
business. That is to say, the undertaking was serious. And it would
prove to be deadly.

ONE

The New World and the Southern Garden

THERE was no "America"—only a few stabs into a long and largely unmapped seacoast—when English explorers began to report on the prospects of settlement in the more southerly regions. It was inevitable that much of this early writing would be promotional literature, calculated bait to lure more adventurers to a new-found land which was still as much legend as fact. The motives behind the drive to colonize an area whose extent could only be guessed at were complex, and it would be risky to judge what drove any individual to make the arduous and frequently costly attempt. English national pride and the promise of importation of raw materials certainly counted; so did the hope of balancing the hold which Spain and Portugal already had in the tropics. There were surely some who saw their mission as lifting the Indians out of savage darkness into Christian light; even more surely there were those who yearned for status and profit much greater than the motherland could proffer. The prospect was often for high drama, in which ordinary people could be raised to heroic roles. For the Puritans of New England, the errand into the wilderness was an act in God's plan for the future of all mankind, and their "city upon a hill" would show the beacon to Christianity everywhere. Further southward, one persistent theme was of Eden regained, a paradise into which the new Adam and his Eve could step at once, free of the burden of a failed past. The serpent had, of course, preceded them; but he was not prominently mentioned.

Early promoters of the New World often misinterpreted or

misrepresented what they saw; they easily drifted into unnatural natural history and a hyperbolic vision of the potentiality of the virgin earth, and these flaws make their "true relations" of dubious value as history or science. But their sheer exuberance, their exclamation of wonder at the strangeness of it all, makes them "literature." All promotional writing has something of this quality, but the southern sun turned some of its creators quite giddy. Here is how Ralph Lane, in 1585 governor of the Roanoke Island colony, rhapsodized over nature's incredible bounty:

We have discovered the maine to bee the goodliest soile under the cope of heaven, so abounding with sweete trees, that bring such sundry rich and most pleasant gummes, grapes of such greatnes, yet wild, as France, Spaine nor Italy hath no greater, so many sortes of Apoethecarie drugs, such severall kinds of flaxe, and one kind like silke. . . . it is the goodliest and most pleasing territorie of the world (for the soile is of a huge unknowen greatnesse, and very wel peopled and towned, though but savagelie) and the climate so wholesome, that we have not had one sicke, since we touched land here.

There is no hint here of the dangers lurking in this "goodliest territorie." Just six years later an English ship discovered that the colonists placed on the island, including the New World's first English infant, Virginia Dare, had vanished into the surrounding wilderness. What they had left behind were a word carved on a tree, the remains of their buildings, and a legend—the "Lost Colony." That over one hundred settlers could disappear so completely is a tantalizing historical mystery in itself; that their identities were so obliterated by the land they were attempting to make theirs supplies a rich theme for national myth. Our history begins with a hiatus; scores of romancers in later years tried to fill it in, even turning Virginia Dare into what one modern scholar has called a "mythic progenitress of American culture."

But the Roanoke tragedy did not slow the heady task of publicizing the new southern plantations during the late sixteenth and early seventeenth centuries. One influential promoter was Thomas Hariot, who had come to the Roanoke settlement with the 1585 expedition. His careful accounts of Indian customs, supplemented with beautiful illustrations by John White, appeared in Europe in four languages. Both helped to establish the image of the red man in foreign eyes for many years. Some of these narratives touch upon topics which in time would come to haunt the national consciousness: the justification of seizing the Indians' lands, the role of the aboriginal both as beast and as noble savage, the prudent use of nature's abundance. Concomitant piety and profit were often lauded. In his sermon-tract called *Good Newes from Virginia* (1613), Alexander Whitaker, a missionary to the colony, exhorts the "right wise and noble adventurers of Virginia" both to carry on God's providential plan in the wilds and to reap the rewards of the earthly paradise. To those who "fight under the banner of Jesus Christ" and "plant his kingdom," he offers a comforting word: "God may defer his temporal reward for a season, but be assured that in the end you shall find riches and honor in this world." He lifts up the hearts of those who might fear scarcity of provender in this wild land: "Wherefore, since God hath filled the elements of earth, air, and water with his creatures, good for our food and nourishment, let not the fear of starving hereafter or of any great want dishearten your valiant minds from coming to a place of so great plenty. If the country were ours, and means for the taking of them (which shortly I hope shall be brought to pass), then all these should be ours." Only a later reader, who knows how efficient would become the instruments for taking these "creatures," could find anything ominous in that phrase of promise: "all these should be ours."

It would be unnatural not to overstate—as does Whitaker— the virtues of a land to which you would draw others; only occasionally does a note of the harsh reality of the colonial experience creep in. Thus the well educated John Pory, who would be the first Speaker of the Virginia General Assembly, writes home to a nobleman of his dreadful sense of isolation from the world of intellect: "At my first coming hither, the solitary uncouthness of this place, compared with those parts of Christendom or Turkey where I had been, and likewise my being sequestered from all occurrents and passages which are so rife there, did not a little vex me." He resolves, though, "being hardened to this custom of abstinence from curiosity," to mind "my business here and, next after my pen, to have some good book always in store, being in solitude the best and choicest company." After all, he acknowledges, there are many advantages in the wild: "Among these crystal rivers and odoriferous woods I do escape much expense, envy, contempt, vanity, and vexation of mind." But Pory finally cannot suppress the pleading note: "Yet, good my lord, have a little compassion upon me and be pleased to send me what pamphlets and relations of the interim since I was with you as Your Lordship shall think good." The plaint of "solitary uncouthness" would echo down the centuries in writing from the South.

The most famous and talented of the promoters of a "new England" was Captain John Smith. His primacy of place rests upon both his efforts in saving the Jamestown colony and his contributions to a fledgling native legendry. Whatever the whole truth of his relationship with Powhatan's daughter, the story of his salvation by Pocahontas has in it the stuff of an archetypical American romance. In recounting it, the brave captain proved he was also a shrewd dramatist; he knew how to stage the sort of exotic scene which would fetch readers yearning for glory and strangeness. His transmutation of the chieftain of a confederation of tribes into an American emperor is done with the flourish of a Renaissance fanfare. As Smith told the tale in his *Generall Historie* (1608), he was brought a captive to a village "where was *Powhatan* their Emperor." His description of the court is reminiscent of those European painters who had limned the barbaric splendor of the New World before any of them had seen it; its action is also like a courtly masque:

Here more than two hundred of those grim Courtiers stood wondering at him, as he had beene a monster; till *Powhatan* and his trayne had put themselves in their greatest braveries. Before a fire upon a seat like a bedsted, he sat covered with a great robe, made of *Rarowcun* skinnes, and all the tayles hanging by. . . . At his entrance before the King, all the people gave a great shout. The Queene of *Appamatuck* was appointed to bring him water to wash his hands, and another brought him a bunch of feathers, in stead of a Towell to dry them: having feasted him after their best barbarous manner they could, a long consultation was held, but the conclusion was, two great stones were brought before *Powhatan:* then as many as could layd hands on him, dragged him to them, and thereon laid his head, and being ready with their clubs, to beat out his braines, *Pocahontas* the Kings dearest daughter, when no intreaty could prevaile, got his head in her armes, and laid her owne upon his to save him from death: whereat the Emperour was contented he should live to make him hatchets, and her bells, beads, and copper.

A rather better fate awaited Captain Smith than such petty artisanship; a more ambiguous destiny lay ahead of Pocahontas. Captured herself in 1613 by the English, who wished to exchange her for some of their own people held by the Indians, she was soon set free, was Christianized as Lady Rebecca, and was married to the colonist John Rolfe. Rolfe's letter to Sir Thomas Dale recounting the reasons for this marriage is not a well known part of the story, but it illuminates the ambivalences in this first formal union of the two races. Rolfe thus lays out his explanation; he had been in "no way led (so farre forth as mans weaknesse may permit) with the unbridled desire of carnall affection; but for the good of this plantation, for the honour of our countrie, for the glory of God, for my owne salvation, and for the converting to the true knowledge of God and Jesus Christ, an unbeleeving creature, namely Pokahuntas."

The marriage was brief but spectacular. In 1616 the couple went to England and were presented to King James I and Queen Anne. Before they could return home Pocahontas died of disease at the age of about twenty-one. She passed quickly into legend. Her contemporaries in Jamestown appear to have believed that she had helped ease tensions between the colonists and the Indians. But her enduring role in national mythology has been as the Indian Queen, an earth goddess of the new land, the innocent primitive noble enough to represent America at a foreign court. Her union with Rolfe and her religious conversion made a connecting bond between two continents and, symbolically, served as a portent of the success of the colonizing mission. Later sentimental literature softened and romanticized her personality. But she left a very real legacy: through her offspring Indian blood flowed into the veins of some of those colonials who would dub themselves "first families." Their ground for pride is self-evident; after all, that blood was "royal." And it was native. In later years the daughters and sons of chiefs of tribes from another continent would find no such acceptance of the fruits of interbreeding.

These early accounts of the collision of Europe with the southern wilderness are worth remembering because they foreshadow some of the themes which would reappear in the more self-conscious literature of the nineteeth-century South. Naive, inaccurate, even devious as they sometimes are, they record the delights and terrors of the colonists as they faced the great wall of the forests. The streets were not paved with gold, but the woods were full of wonders. No one would encounter men whose heads did grow beneath their shoulders, but there were exotic flora and fauna which raised the prospect of marvels yet to come. One can empathize with Alexander Whitaker as he first looked upon one of these "strange beasts," the "female possum, which will let forth her young out of her belly and take them up into her belly again at her pleasure without hurt to herself. Neither think this to be a traveller's tale but the very truth, for nature hath framed her fit for that service; my eyes have been witness unto it."

As the colonies grew and prospered in the seventeenth century, writing would become more matter-of-fact, more "civilized." Though there are few printed documents from this period, some religious texts, including plain-style sermons, have survived. Letter-writing flourished. Political tracts and oratory were inevitably a product of the developing social structure of the colonial system; and documents by the score record speeches, proclamations, dealings with the Indians, surveys, charges to juries, and the like. There was no printing establishment beyond the local gazettes and no real pressure for one, since widespread distribution of materials would have been quite impractical.

Yet the colonials were not without a desire for reading matter. Records of early libraries and booksellers show that their taste for fiction, plays, and poetry was quite like that of the homeland. Some circulated their own verses and other compositions in manuscript among friends, but such activity clearly was considered an avocation. The literature of New England is enriched by the poetry of Anne Bradstreet and Edward Taylor, but scholars have found no similar tradition of religious verse in the southern colonies. Though the settler would become obsessive about many aspects of the southern scene, his formal religion was not one of them.

Full evaluation of writing in the southern colonies has been hampered both because many records were destroyed and because the great mass of documents long remained in manuscript. Only in recent years have students working in neglected archives been able to refute the dogmatic conclusion of older historians that the region lacked a literature of any consequence. Further exhumation will enable us better to understand the relationship of that literature to a developing southern cultural tradition.

Much of what the South would come to think of as its "aristocratic" way of life was created during the eighteenth century. As the frontier crept westward, the tidewater regions began to take on the tone of a settled and stratified, though still largely rural, society. With a greater influx of immigrants, with the development of slavery, and with a flourishing economy based on production of tobacco in the upper regions and rice and indigo in the lower, a more gracious manner of living became possible for many. There was as yet no King Cotton and no King Cotton mentality, with its dream of a slave-based empire, but it was not unthinkable for a James River planter to consider himself at least the equal of an English country squire. A remarkable example of this rise in status was William Byrd II of Westover.

Born in Virginia in 1674, Byrd was sent by his father, who had once been an Indian trader, to be educated in English schools; and, like many a son of the South after him, he studied law at the Middle Temple. During his London years he became an adept at sexual adventuring; but he lusted equally for recognition by the English ruling classes—and he succeeded. His acquaintanceship with playwrights like Wycherley and Congreve attests to his love of the stage; his association with titled men like the Earl of Orrery and the Duke of Argyll suggests an infatuation with the more realistic theater of politics. Never a man to play the insecure colonial, Byrd made his friendships pay. Under the sponsorship of Sir Robert Southwell, he was elected to the Royal Society at the age of twenty-two. Byrd returned briefly to Virginia and was a member of the House of Burgesses, but by 1697 he was back in England as colonial agent. He was never to attain some of his higher ambitions—to be governor of Virginia or of Maryland—but his services on behalf of the colony in which he actually spent only about half of his seventy years were indeed remarkable. He would be surprised that the historian of southern letters now finds his literary activity equally notable.

Byrd returned permanently to his Westover home in 1726 and

spent much of his time managing his estates in Virginia and North Carolina. He also collected a library of some 4,000 volumes, one of the choicest and largest in all the colonies. He had always been a voracious reader in several languages, and he had dabbled in the literary forms in vogue during his London days: the character sketch, verse, letter-writing. But his greatest legacy to southern— and national—literature was to be concealed during his lifetime. The principal work, *The History of the Dividing Line betwixt Virginia and North Carolina run in the Year of Our Lord 1728*, was not published until 1841, when selections were printed from the Westover manuscripts. Byrd may have demurred about sending it to press because he felt it lacked final polishing or because of a gentlemanly punctilio about a public performance; only a few of his contemporaries in Virginia and England were permitted to peruse the manuscript. Basically an account, as the title states, of Byrd's leadership of a commission appointed to settle a boundary dispute, the narrative is also a contribution to nascent southern humor as well as to history and natural science. Another intriguing aspect, in view of his region's later attitude toward racial interbreeding, is Byrd's argument for miscegenation as a way of resolving the Indian problem. Though there is an ironical tone in several of his sentences, his remarks on the reasons for the whites' lack of success in converting the Indians sound quite seriously meant:

For my part, I must be of opinion, as I hinted before, that there is but one way of converting these poor infidels and reclaiming them from barbarity, and that is charitably to intermarry with them . . . . Had the English done this at the first settlement of the colony, the infidelity of the Indians had been worn out at this day with their dark complexions, and the country had swarmed with people more than it does with insects. It was certainly an unreasonable nicety that prevented their entering into so good-natured an alliance. All nations of men have the same natural dignity, and we all know that very bright talents may be lodged under a very dark skin. The principal difference between one people and another proceeds only from the different opportunities of improvement. The Indians by no means want understanding and are in their figure tall and well proportioned. Even their copper-colored complexion would admit of blanching, if not in the first, at the farthest in the second, generation. I may safely venture to say, the Indian women would have made altogether as honest wives for the first planters as the damsels they used to purchase from aboard the ships. 'Tis strange, therefore, that any good Christian should have refused a wholesome straight bedfellow, when he might have had so far a portion with her as the merit of saving her soul.

Racy, colloquial, frequently witty, observant, *The History of the Dividing Line* is now generally recognized as a landmark in colonial literature. What is probably an earlier version is called *The Secret History of the Line;* it is a shorter narrative which likely was designed for a select group of readers, since it satirizes Byrd's companions on the expedition, especially the Carolinians. North Carolinians rarely figure well in Byrd's writings; indeed, in a notable passage in the *History*, they are reduced to inhabitants of "Lubberland." The report surely betrays the class consciousness of one who had known a royal court. Byrd obviously delighted in composing this first extended portrait of that perennial target of disdain and amusement, the shiftless poor white:

The men, for their parts, just like the Indians, impose all the work upon the poor women. They make their wives rise out of their beds early in the morning, at the same time that they lie and snore till the sun has risen one-third of his course and dispersed all the unwholesome damps. Then, after stretching and yawning for half an hour, they light their pipes, and, under the protection of a cloud of smoke, venture out into the open air; though if it happen to be never so little cold they quickly return shivering into the chimney corner. When the weather is mild, they stand leaning with both arms upon the cornfield fence and gravely consider whether they had best go and take a small heat at the hoe but generally find reasons to put it off till another time. Thus they loiter away their lives, like Solomon's sluggard, with their arms across, and at the winding up of the year scarcely have bread to eat.

Byrd's pithy observation is also characteristic of his other major essays, *A Progress to the Mines* and *A Journey to the Land of Eden*. However, his secret diary, more akin in spirit to that of Samuel Pepys of London than of Samuel Sewall of New England, is mechanically written and displays little of Pepys's literary grace. It is, nonetheless, a unique record of the large planter's daily life, and it tells us far more than would a formal autobiography about the sexual mores of the time and place. Byrd was not directly to influence the growing literature of the South, since his manuscripts did not reach a large audience until they were printed in the nineteenth and twentieth centuries. But they provide us with a clear notion of an otherwise sparsely documented region and period. They also show the growing discontent with the mother country among the landed gentry. For all his long residence in England, his social climbing, and his pleasure in the court, Byrd was proud of his rank as a Virginia gentleman and large landholder. The division between England and its dominion was beginning to gain force. We are fortunate that such a clear-eyed man as Byrd was on hand to set it down.

The more formal histories of the colonies, written now by men who had been born in them, also disclose this developing sense of the independent rights of colonials and their increasing pride in past achievements. Byrd's brother-in-law, Robert Beverley, is a good example of chroniclers who were seeing the native scene with native eyes. In his *History and Present State of Virginia*, published in 1705 and revised in 1722, he waxes as enthusiastic as did his predecessors over the natural abundance of the colony, and, like Byrd, he laments that the early settlers did not intermarry with the Indians in order to avoid racial conflicts. Beverley's book shows an attempt to create a native prose; with some justice, it has been called the first self-consciously American history of a southern colony.

It was soon to be supplemented by the work of an English clergyman, Hugh Jones, who taught at the College of William and Mary and served as rector of several parishes. In *The Present State of Virginia* (1724), Jones set down some early observations on the slave system: "The Negroes are very numerous, some gentlemen having hundreds of them of all sorts, to whom they bring great profit; for the sake of which they are obliged to keep them well, and not overwork, starve, or famish them, besides other inducements to favour them; which is done in a great degree, to such especially that are laborious, careful and honest; though indeed some masters, careless of their own interest or reputation, are too cruel and negligent." The notion of the blacks' foreordained role to be servants and workers only is explicit in his further comment: "Several of them are taught to be sawyers, carpenters, smiths, coopers, etc. and though for the most part they be none of the aptest or nicest; yet they are by nature cut out for hard labour and fatigue, and will perform tolerably well; though they fall much short of an Indian, that has learned and seen the same things; and those Negroes make the best servants, that have been slaves in their own country; for they that have been kings and great men there are generally lazy, haughty, and obstinate."

Jones is rather sharp about some traits of the white Virginians which would become clichés in later literature, above all their nonintellectual bent:

Thus they have good natural notions, and will soon learn arts and sciences; but are generally diverted by business or inclination from profound study, and prying into the depths of things . . . .

They are more inclinable to read men by business and conversation than to dive into books, and are for the most part only desirous of learning what is absolutely necessary, in the shortest and best method.

This is the voice of Professor Jones, the Oxonian charged at William and Mary with the instruction of young gentlemen. Another voice, that of the Anglican divine and colonial rector, appears in his praise of Virginia as the golden mean in American religion: "If New England be called a receptacle of dissenters, and an Amsterdam of religion, Pennsylvania the nursery of Quakers, Maryland the retirement of Roman Catholicks, North Carolina the refuge of run-aways, and South Carolina the delight of buccaneers and pyrates, Virginia may be justly esteemed the happy retreat of true Britons and true churchmen for the most part; neither soaring too high nor drooping too low, consequently should merit the greater esteem and encouragement."

The lower southern colonies produced only a small amount of historical writing, the most notable of which is John Lawson's *A New Voyage to Carolina* (1709). As much promotional treatise as history, it emphasizes the great natural potential of the region. It also presents a poignant view of the Indians, one that acknowledges the guilt of the whites in eradicating their culture:

They are really better to us, than we are to them; they always give us Victuals at their Quarters and take care we are arm'd against Hunger and Thirst: We do not so by them (generally speaking) but let them walk by our Doors Hungry, and do not often relieve them. We look upon them with Scorn and Disdain, and think them little better than Beasts in Humane Shape, though if well examined, we shall find that, for all our Religion and Education, we possess more Moral Deformities, and Evils than these Savages do, or are acquainted withal.

We reckon them Slaves in Comparison to us, and Intruders, as oft as they enter our Houses, or hunt near our Dwellings. But if we will admit Reason to be our Guide, she will inform us, that these *Indians* are the freest People in the World, and so far from being Intruders upon us, that we have abandon'd our own Native Soil, to drive them out, and possess theirs.

Such sympathy would be rare in later decades. Ironically, while on an exploratory mission in North Carolina in 1711, Lawson was captured by Indians, tortured, and put to death.

These early authors occasionally betray their sense of personal distance from a land which, to echo Robert Frost, they possessed without yet being possessed by. Identification with the soil was to increase during the eighteenth century; and with the consciousness that they were building a culture they began to produce a much more urbane polite literature. That much of this prose and verse was derivative, that too often it was merely a feeble shadow of fashionable British models, is a conventional observation. What is remarkable is that in a still rustic region, without a single dominant cultural center, so many wrote so much as well as they did. Much of this material, of course, existed only in manuscript, especially personal journals and letters. But the printing press was now established in towns in South Carolina, Virginia, and Maryland; and the "Gazettes" frequently carried belletristic contributions as well as news. We would expect the essays dealing with agriculture, education, and politics; we might be more surprised at the quite respectable efforts in the manner of the British *Spectator*. The gentlemanly pose of such authors is characteristic; they simply offered effusions struck off in idle hours. Verse-writing flourished in all the English colonies; in the southern region it tended less toward the religious (though one finds examples of elegies, epitaphs, and hymns) than toward the elegant and satirical. Modern anthologies illustrate a quite wide range, from graceful tributes to the ladies to patriotic praising of the countryside. Most of these are relatively short. A notable extended satire is Ebenezer Cooke's (or Cook's) *The Sot-Weed Factor* (i.e., tobacco broker), which is a mocking survey of Chesapeake Bay culture in the early 1700s. A sample of his generally splenetic style is this depiction of the Maryland capital:

> Up to *Annapolis* I went,
> A City Situate on a plain,
> Where scarce a House will keep out Rain;
> The Buildings fram'd with Cyprus rare,
> Resembles much our *Southwark* Fair:
> But Stranger here will scarcely meet
> With Market-place, Exchange, or Street;
> And if the Truth I may report,
> 'Tis not so large as *Tottenham Court.*

Probably true enough, but one doubts that Cooke had the opportunity to authenticate the allegations of one scurrilous couplet: "May Wrath Divine then lay those Regions wast / Where no Man's Faithful, nor a Woman Chast."

The culminating glory of southern colonial literature is, of course, the political writing of the Revolutionary generation. Because the papers and speeches of statesmen like James Madison and Thomas Jefferson loom so large in the history of the whole nation, it is not easy to see in them specifically regional influences. Certainly rhetorical skill and emotional flourish were not peculiar to the southern landholders. But decades of fighting for the rights of the colonists had forced upon the planter class a leadership role which helped to bring the United States into being. Southerners' skill in debate, their experience as legislators, their ability to discern subtle distinctions in the law would still be characteristic traits on the eve of the Civil War.

The colonial and the early national years left to the southern region a peculiar legacy: slavery and a strong agrarian point of view. The inexhaustible fecundity of the land had been trumpeted from the earliest days; a people were now firmly rooted in that land. A complex production and trade system had been established. The wealthier planter families had developed a sense of rank within a caste system; clanship had been formed by intermarriage within class. The southern region had a distinctive "tone," which had been remarked upon during the debates which led to the proclamation of independence. "Yankee" and "southern gentleman" were even more recognizable types at the end of the Revolution. But certainly regionalism in the broader sense was not yet a fact; primary loyalty was still to the state, as once it had been to the colony. The area was too vast and geographically diverse to be conceived of as an integral unit. Such physical conditions could not be altered in the decades before 1860; what *did* change, though, under the necessity of defending the common rights of a disparate people, was a condition of mind.

TWO

The Growth of
Southern Separatism

THE PRESSURES culminating in the assertion of nationhood, the dynamics of a separatist outlook, can never be fully comprehended. Individual beliefs—the unit ideas which fuse into a complex whole —may be tabulated; the why of their being is less easy to determine. What happened in the South between the creation of the United States and the formation of the Confederacy is one of the great dramas of the habitation of the North American continent. But who wrote the script? How were the actors assembled and how did they realize their roles? One overwhelming fact confronts us: southerners had been leaders in the struggle to free all the colonies; to the new nation they contributed four of the first five presidents. But only thirty-five years after the death of Thomas Jefferson his own Virginia and ten other states were to assert their right to leave the union. The success of the creation of "the South" had a grimly pragmatic test: tens of thousands died for its preservation. The mythos was strong enough to survive even the Civil War which ended its corporate entity. The South did not have to "rise again"; in many senses it never died.

A dispassionate observer in the early nineteenth century might well have concluded that the likelihood was remote that the individualistic southerner could come to identify with a nationalistic cause. For one thing, except for the seacoast, the boundaries of the region were ill defined. The coastal plain blended into the piedmont; the piedmont rose into the highland mass of the Appalachians; beyond the mountains lay arable lands that extended to the Mississippi—and who knew how far beyond? Moreover, the people were already a heterogeneous ethnic mix. Those of English stock still dominated the coastal areas, but into the piedmont and the mountains had come the Scotch-Irish and the Germans. Pockets of an even more exotic French and Spanish culture were still observable in the deepest south. Religion was as diversified as the people who had brought it. Pride in an old gentry was notable mainly in Virginia and South Carolina; elsewhere the mass of the people lived a countrified life of limited social horizons. There were many prosperous farmers, but there were also the squatters on hardscrabble lands left by the advance westward. The cultural scene was unpromising; there were no very large cities, no dominant center for the arts, no major libraries, no colleges deserving of the name, no publishers who had the capacity for the wide distribution of local writings.

Most notably, there were clashing opinions about the future of slavery. During the Virginia debates on the issue, which succeeded the Nat Turner insurrection of 1831, many southerners accepted the idea that a gradual and peaceful emancipation might be achieved. But the forces of moderation weakened as the voice of the abolitionists grew louder; manumission was proclaimed as an evil when the proslavery forces began to fall back upon the "positive good" theory of Negro bondage. By the 1850s nearly all leading voices of southern opinion were citing the natural hierarchy of the universe, the testimony of ancient writers, ethnology, and the authority of the Bible as evidence of the inestimable benefit to the slave's body and soul of the "peculiar institution." How did it happen? Given such diversity as this brief summation suggests, who could imagine an entity called "the South," a new nation insisting on its own manifest destiny?

It was imagined—and effected—with astonishing celerity and efficiency. Some stages are clear. The Missouri Compromise of 1820 recognized the admission of new slave and free states into the union, thus perpetuating an internal division. The problem of maintaining this balance became an obsession with many southern leaders. After about 1830 the region south of the Potomac grew more clamorous about the principle of states' rights; it went on the defensive. Historians suggest a number of reasons for this increasing withdrawal from the rest of the nation. The economic factor is plain. The earlier South had depended upon several staple crops, especially tobacco, rice, and indigo. Such crops did not require vast space and did not necessitate a large labor pool. The invention of the cotton gin, the mounting dependence of a huge area upon a single staple crop, the depletion of soil which attended its culture, and the enormous force necessary to work the cotton lands—all these elements had far-reaching effects. They would commit the South to a continued agrarian base; they would also make the fate of the black people inevitable. Much of what the South perceived as evil in the North's development of finance capitalism deserved criticism; a good New Englander like Henry Thoreau would also denounce it as corrupting. But the South's concomitant defense of its own labor system drove it into moral ambiguity. It would have to argue that the ends, a thriving and ordered society, fully justified the means, a slave-based economy. It would also have to maintain that a slave-holding people could sustain a culture at least equal to that of the industrialized North. The political and economic argument proved a pragmatic success; the argument for cultural equality was voiced vociferously, but its very stridency proclaimed its failure. The South demanded local periodicals to disseminate its views; it got them—and would not underwrite them. It demanded patriotic novelists, poets, playwrights; it got them—and would not support them.

Why was there such disparity between promise and actual patronage? The answer is not easy to come by. But one way to get at the relationship between the creators of the body politic and the creators of a nationalistic literature is to survey the contents of one of the more prestigious magazines. It is here that we may best begin to sample the atmosphere in which antebellum southern authors had to live, and tried to do their work.

Though never voracious readers, southerners did subscribe to both northern and British periodicals in fair numbers. The desire to create southern counterparts was one facet of growing nationalistic sentiment; it seemed obvious that local writers should have outlets of their own in order to refute outsiders' sneers at the paucity of native talent. This was a reasonable assumption on the face of it, but editors and proprietors always overestimated the hunger of their countrymen for their products. Professionalism—actually being paid for literary work—still had something of a taint on it. Southern magazinists deserved far better of their compatriots than they ever received. They extolled the beauties of the scene, defended local institutions, voiced the nobler aspirations of their people, gave form to the dreams of a more perfect society. They lashed out at the North and its still dominating culture; they tried to create a sense of solidarity among a people who, they argued, were coming to have a common aim. Farm journals and economic reviews did have a fair success; probably their editors could better judge what readers actually wanted. But the many literary quarterlies and monthlies issued in these antebellum decades tended to die at a very young age, with little lapse between the dates of their founding and their foundering. Only the *Southern Literary Messenger* (1834–1864) managed to last through the high years of the Old South. Because of its relatively long run and because it is an exemplar of the best and the worst of the magazine world, it is worth an extended examination. No other periodical gives one so clear an insight into the trials of southern authorship and editorship.

Founded in Richmond in 1834 by T. W. White, the *Messenger* would publish contributions by nearly all in the South who could call themselves authors and many who did not deserve the name. In its earlier years, it also welcomed the work of northerners, even though they, unlike most of their southern brethren, expected to be paid. The first number appeared in August 1834 and was prefaced by a notice from White's hand. Introducing a series of encomiums he had solicited from notables of both sections, he urged that their sentiments "ought to stimulate the pride and genius of the south, and awaken from its long slumber the literary exertion of this portion of our country." Washington Irving gratifyingly expressed himself as strongly disposed "in favor of 'the south,' and especially attached to Virginia." James Fenimore Cooper thought the South "full of talent," but quite erroneously he supposed that "the leisure of its gentlemen ought to enable them to bring it freely into action." James Kirke Paulding also foresaw that many a Virginia lass or lad would spring forward with their "effusions"; and he sounded an inspirational note: "If your young writers will consult their own taste and genius, and forget there ever were such writers as Scott, Byron, and Moore, I will be bound they produce something original. . . . Give us something new—something characteristic of yourselves, your country, and your native feelings, and I don't care what it is. I am somewhat tired of licentious love ditties, border legends, affected sorrows, and grumbling misanthropy. I want to see something wholesome, natural, and national." "Grumbling misanthropy" rarely darkened the souls of the *Messenger*'s contributors, and their love ditties fastidiously eschewed the licentious; otherwise, Paulding's sound advice might have been written on the wind.

The editorial which immediately followed these quoted messages of goodwill was by the first (and, naturally, unpaid) editor, James E. Heath. Headed simply "Southern Literature," it tried a few bugle notes: "Hundreds of similar publications thrive and prosper north of the Potomac, sustained as they are by the liberal hand of patronage. *Shall not one be supported in the whole South?* . . . Are we to be doomed forever to a kind of vassalage to our northern neighbors—a dependence for our literary food upon our brethren, whose superiority in all the great points of character,—in valor—eloquence and patriotism, we are no wise disposed to admit?" Heath's tone grew more shrill as he faced the annoying reality. How was it, he asked, that in such a large state, with "a vast deal of agricultural wealth, and innumerable persons of both sexes, who enjoy both leisure and affluence," there was not "one solitary periodical exclusively literary?" A note of ethnic superiority began to creep in as Heath continued his breast-beating:

Why should we consider the worthy descendants of the pilgrims—of the Hollanders of Manhattan, or the German adventurers of Pennsylvania, as exclusively entitled to cater for us in our choicest intellectual aliment? Shall it be said that the empire of literature has no geographical boundaries, and that local jealousies ought not to disturb its harmony? . . . If we continue to be *consumers* of northern productions, we shall never ourselves become *producers*. We may take from them the fabrics of their looms, and give in exchange without loss our agricultural products—but if we depend exclusively upon their *literary* supplies, it is certain that the spirit of invention among our own sons, will be damped, if not entirely extinguished.

In what would be a recurring note in southern periodicals, the editor concluded with a plea for funds—support which would work "towards the creation of a new era in the annals of this blessed Old Dominion. It may possibly be the means of effecting a salutary reform in public taste and individual habits; of overcoming that tendency to mental repose and luxurious indulgence supposed to be peculiar to southern latitudes; and of awakening a spirit of inquiry and a zeal for improvement, which cannot fail ultimately to exalt and adorn society."

Noble rhetoric—but unhappily undercut by the very first contribution to the *Messenger*, which immediately succeeded the editor's words: one of those dismal "Extracts from a Journal" which padded out pages without supplying either pleasure or light. In this case, it was "from the unpublished journal of a gentleman of this state, who visited Europe some years since." The editor probably intended a gentlemanly tone of modest deprecation and not honest evaluation when he noted that the piece was presented without "any peculiar claims to admiration," but the contributor was just as good as his billing. It took him five paragraphs and three quotations just to get out of sight of land.

The early issues of the *Messenger* suggest that its publisher was more concerned with establishing a literature written by southerners than with encouraging a specifically regional bias in its content. Perhaps White had actually expected that the supposititious "leisure class" would now eagerly put polished pens at his disposal; if so, he must have been disappointed by the torpor of the Muse. His more regular local contributors turned out to be not planters and their gracious ladies but members of the professional classes—lawyers, physicians, educators, clergymen. The prose which they produced is often an index of *their* taste; not so often, one may guess, was it that of their readers. Their style, in the literary tradition of a generation that was already passing, was ponderous, rhetorical, studded with classical allusions and poetic tags; their subjects were scarcely rousers. Of course there was a lighter side. Though the first editor professed a distaste for the Gothic and the sentimental, he put up with pallid imitations of Scott and the "German school." The poetry department was just as derivative, with the early British romantics as favorite models. Like Mark Twain's Emmeline Grangerford, the teenage poetess so admired by Huck Finn, these versifiers could write about almost anything, "just so it was sadful." It is easy to mock the sentimental posturings of another age, though it is hard to do so with the wit of a Twain. The truth is that such verse was in vogue in both North and South—indeed the North's Lydia Huntley Sigourney was a regular (and paid) contributor to the *Messenger*. But readers of a later day have forever (one hopes) lost the ability to empathize with the lines of these empty-headed warblers.

White doubtless would have been willing to pay something to southern contributors had the budget allowed it. But most of what money there was had to be disbursed to northern professionals whose names lent as much tone to his journal as did their offerings. Southerners were expected to try to match them in the name of southern pride. But amateurs are apt to write amateurishly, and they have little patience with those who tell them that they labor in vain. Unhappily White himself had little talent for literary evaluation, and he duly printed their lucubrations, their "lines," their dim little tales, their leaves from travel journals. What, one wonders, did he throw away?

For some fourteen months in its early days the *Messenger* suddenly took on a more mature, more worldly tone under the editorial supervision of a young aspiring professional, Edgar Allan Poe. Poe came with the recommendation of John Pendleton Kennedy, a Baltimore man of letters who had recently made a name for himself with *Swallow Barn,* a sketchbook of Virginia life. White never liked Poe (his drinking habits only topped the list of the proprietor's complaints against him) but the fact is that his young assistant singlehandedly increased the *Messenger's* subscription list and brought it to national attention. Poe contributed not only a number of his early tales and poems; he also created (and largely wrote) a lively and perceptive book review section. He was not always scrupulous in his reviewing; he paraded learning filched from encyclopedias and other sources, he padded out his pieces with long quotations from the material under consideration, and he was niggling about points which others thought irrelevant. He often used his pen as a dart, piercing tender and tough sensibilities with equal skill. White had not wanted controversy of this sort in his journal, but his main complaint was that Poe aimed South as well as North, taking on not only the prominent New York novelist Theodore Fay but also the South's premier literary man, William Gilmore Simms. Poe assumed his duties in December 1835; in January 1837, after numerous squabbles with the publisher, he was fired for good. Poe had been miserably paid for his considerable toil, but White had found him no bargain.

With his departure from Richmond for New York, Poe left the southern literary scene forever. But his stint on the *Messenger* raises a question that has long vexed literary historians: how "southern" a writer was Poe? In most discussions, a positive or negative conclusion usually rests upon the stake which the critic has in "proving" his case. For the facts are equivocal. It is true that Poe spent most of his early years in the South; he attended the University of Virginia for a brief period; he began his literary career by winning a prize in Baltimore, where he had relatives; he achieved renown if not always admiration on the *Messenger*; he held racist views; he yearningly aspired to the status of "gentleman." Moreover, his taste in verse was formed in the South, and he fashioned his own work on approved models. His criticism very likely owes something to his studies during his few months at the university. But in the body of his tales and poems only a few can be associated with a southern locale, and even in these he evinces little interest in evoking a sense of real place. Perhaps the question may be put in perspective by speculating on what Poe might have done had he remained on the *Messenger* under a more congenial proprietorship. It is not likely that he would have had much enthusiasm for the *Messenger*'s increasingly sectional stance. Politics, except of the literary variety, was of little concern to him. His own driving ambition was to become the Artist in America, the man dedicated to a craft free of the "heresy of the didactic." Such an ambition demanded a wider stage than that of a provincial southern town; it required the arena of a national center like New York or Philadelphia. A "southerner" through early experience Poe undoubtedly was; but a "southern writer" would have been too mediocre a title for him.

Poe's flight to the North suggests something of the continuing dilemma which the proprietor of a southern literary journal faced during the 1830s and 1840s. However rich the hidden genius of Virginia and its sister states, it did not overexert itself in the *Mes-*

senger. To survive, the journal needed a more national audience, and, after Poe's departure, White went on wooing northern writers and subscribers, who were always less stingy with their talents and their dollars. The drive for a native literature was thus compromised; but, as White often reminded them, his compatriots had mainly themselves to blame. The New Year editorial for January 1838 again sounded what was becoming a wearisome theme: "There exists southward of the Potomac, a mass of *cultivated* mind sufficient, with only a little industry and care in practising the art of composition, to fill twenty such magazines as this, with instruction and delight." There is obvious frustration behind White's apostrophe to "the conscious possessor of talent"—"we say to him " 'WRITE.' "

White was also beginning to be bedevilled by another problem which the *Messenger* could scarcely overlook: the spectre of slavery. In keeping with its situation in Richmond, it had run proslavery pieces; in keeping with the "literary" emphasis in its title and in its effort not to rile northern readers, it had endeavored to avoid the "ultra" tone. But by 1841 White was compelled to assert that direct attacks on his homeland required direct response; the *Messenger* must be "the medium for the defence and exposition of *Southern* interests and *Southern* rights." White died two years later, but his journal managed to live on, though often precariously, for twenty-one more years. Trying to be both "southern" and "literary", its succeeding editors steered it on a wavering course. After merging in 1845 with Simms's *Southern and Western Monthly Magazine and Review,* it announced that it aimed to be "truly Southern and Western, but without being anti-Northern." The stance was, of course, impossible to maintain.

For a time the journal concentrated heavily on the early history of Virginia, in a nostalgic attempt to resurrect the glories of the Ancient Dominion. Fiction, though, was not entirely neglected; regional tales appeared, as did a serialization of Beverley Tucker's third novel, *Gertrude.* And, as always, there were those self-pitying and pitiable "stanzas." By the end of the 1840s the long campaign to lure native contributors seemed to be paying off. The *Messenger* regularly ran Philip Pendleton Cooke's stories of the Virginia frontier and even that renegade son of Virginia, Poe, sent in several items. But there was still the old trouble; by August

1850, editor John R. Thompson, citing the trials of J. D. B. De Bow in operating his *Commercial Review,* had to lash out again at fickle supporters:

We have exerted ourselves in vain to awaken a worthy sectional spirit, which should emulate the works of our Northern brethren—we have cried ourselves hoarse in calls upon Southern pride to throw off the slavish literary yoke of New England—we have appealed to no purpose in moments of urgent necessity even for the payment of our just dues; the response has generally been such as Mr. De Bow chronicles, stopping the magazine and sending it back with postage, leaving us to cry out in the broken-hearted accents of the rejected swain.

> Perhaps it was right to dissemble your love,
> But why did you kick me downstairs?

The wry reference to rascally subscribers might have amused T. W. White; but what would this first editor, who had endeavored not to let the slavery issue overwhelm the "literary" aspects of his magazine, have made of the lead article in the October 1856 issue? Entitled "The Duty of Southern Authors," it begins with the expected moan: "If there is any wish for the accomplishment of which we could breathe forth our most earnest prayers, it is for the establishment of a *Southern* literature, standing secure and independent upon its own pedestal, lighting up the threshold of its temple with the refulgent beams of its self-illumination." The author goes on, with ruffles and flourishes, to a high-toned vindication of literary endeavor as that which gives a people "a position among the nations of the earth." Well and good, but what is the *duty* of the southern author? The second paragraph gives the game away:

While it is the imperative duty of the authors of *all* nations to let the light shine that God has given them—to contribute, like so many springs, to swell the great stream of human knowledge and happiness, till it overflows its banks with the waters of truth—to worship wisdom and learning for their own sakes—while such motives, and such promptings as these, should inspire the heart, and kindle the genius of *every* author; yet to the *Southern* writer, besides all these, there should be other inducements and incentives to literary labors. Graver and more solemn considerations than a mere thirst for fame and distinction, should impel him to drive his pen. He lives in a community where African slavery subsists.

The modern reader, lulled by the cadenced jargon of the first part of the passage, may experience a shock when he hits that last sentence. It is, however, the burden of the article, as it is to be the burden of the southern author; one must write in the service of that community. Ignorance of the slave system in the South has caused the world to be arrayed against it. The spectre of *Uncle Tom's Cabin* rises above the words as the writer whips on his brethren:

As literature has been the most powerful weapon which the enemies of African slavery have used in their attacks, so, also, to literature we must look for the maintenance of our position, and our justification before the world. Let Southern authors, men who see and know slavery as it is, make it their duty to deluge all the realms of literature with a flood of light upon this subject. Let them dispel with the sun of genius the mists and clouds which ignorance and fanaticism have thrown around slavery, purposely involving it in an obscurity and darkness, through which men will not grope to find the truths upon which it reposes. This, then, is the "Duty of Southern Authors."

Some of the obstacles to fulfilling such patriotic exhortation were explored in the *Messenger*'s next issue, in a screed called "An Inquiry into the Present State of Southern Literature." Its tone is less strident, but its message is similar: southern authors simply have not stood up to challenge the anti-southern and antislavery sentiments which fill the textbooks and literary works which flood in from the North. The list of horrors is headed by the histories of George Bancroft, which are said to feed southern children anti-slavery poison with no local antidote on hand. Nor are fiction and poetry less threatening. Predictably, Mrs. Stowe is savaged, but so is that gentle bard Longfellow, who—regretfully—has to be recognized as "the first of our living American poets." He can be praised so long as "his muse devotes herself to her true mission of interpreting the kinder feelings of the heart," as in "Excelsior" or "Evangeline" or "Hiawatha." But this "tender minstrel" has perverted his genius to the south's injury: "He too must administer in the attractive draught of his poetry the poison of abolition." One has to lay down his works with a sigh " at finding that one whom we had loved to recognize as a brother, nourishes in his heart a fraternity like that of Cain."

After some more scattered fire, the author gets down to his point: why has the South failed to fence out this subversive northern influx? First, he argues, the South has been forced to devote its greatest talents to politics and has driven them away from polite learning: "A period of political agitation, or of civil strife, is not a period for the cultivation of Belles Lettres." Moreover, too many sons of the South have been seeking "their fortune in some new home in the far West," thereby preventing "that growth of population which is essential to the maintenance of a home literature." Is there, then, any hope for southern letters? The writer finds it primarily in better southern support for local— and doctrinaire— education: "We doubt whether all other causes combined have done more essential injury to the prosperity of the South than the neglect of her colleges for Northern institutions." But scarcely less important, the article concludes, is the encouragement of native periodicals; with no visible blush the *Southern Literary Messenger* is named the best of breed.

The claims for the slumbering genius of the southern people which the *Messenger* had long supported were to undergo severe critical examination in its last horrendous years from 1860 to 1864. Having grown, along with the homeland which it represented, more isolated from the wider cultural realm, it offered in its editorial comment an increasingly delusory—indeed, almost hallucinatory—interpretation of the South's past, present, and future. Just how far the *Messenger* had moved out of a prideful regionalism into a paranoid ethnocentricity can be observed in an article which appeared in June 1860. Entitled "The Difference of Race Between the Northern and Southern People," it is, in essence, a compendium of the nonsensical ideas that had been evolving over the past decades—what we now know as "the Cavalier myth." In the development of this romantic nationalism, politicians, clergymen, historians, and, as we shall see, fiction writers had played an important role; how well they had wrought, this essay grimly illustrates.

The opening proposition is simply stated: America is and has been from the settlement two nations:

The Northern States were originally settled by disaffected religionists, under charters from the government of England, and these people belong to the true Saxon stock, as found in the country when invaded by the Normans. . . .

On the other hand, the Southern States were settled and governed, in a great measure, under the supervision of the crown, immediately by and under the direction of persons belonging to the blood and race of the reigning family, and belonged to that stock recognized as CAVALIERS—who were the *royalists* in the time of Charles I., the commonwealth, and Charles II., and directly descended from the Norman Barons of William the Conqueror, a race distinguished, in its earliest history, for its warlike and fearless character, a race, in all time since, renowned for its gallantry, its chivalry, its honour, its gentleness and its intellect. . . . The Southern people come of that race . . . to whom law and order, obedience and command, are convertible terms, and who *do* command, the world over, whether the subject be African or Caucasian, Celt or Saxon.

These ethnic origins account for the irreconcilable differences in mind and character between North and South:

In intellect, [Northerners] are vigourous, inventive and discursive,— in character they are devotional, and contentious, with but little appreciation of a delicate and honourable sensibility. . . . having liberty which they do not appreciate, they run into anarchy,—being devotional, they push their piety to the extremes of fanaticism,—being contentious withal, they are led to attack the interests of others, merely because those interests do not comport with *their* ideas of right.

On the contrary, the Southern mind . . . is disposed to quiet and to gentleness, coming to conclusions by the almost instinctive application of the simplest rules,—yet when roused to action, capable of almost incredible effort, and equal to the highest flight of genius. Naturally generous, Southrons exercise much forbearance, till the question of honour is raised, and then they rush to the sword,—accustomed to enforce obedience when it is due, they readily yield it when their position and duty require it,—fierce and fearless in a contest, yet just, generous and gentle in command,—they possess every quality necessary to rule the Northern people; to establish rules of justice between the rights of the two people, and to preserve the government. The which, if they fail now to perform, they are false to the instincts of the NORMAN RACE.

The gauntlet was at last down; just six months after these provocative words appeared, South Carolina left the Union.

In the waning years of wartime the *Messenger*'s editorial comment focussed upon several interlinked themes: (1) the South had not fully appreciated how it had let the North dictate national standards of literature and art; (2) though there had never been a deficiency of literary talent, the South simply had not supported its own people and had driven many to seek publication in the North; (3) the war, by forcing southerners to deep self-examination, had finally wakened the consciousness of the Confederacy to the need for a literature worthy of its blood and military zeal. In October 1863, just three months after the Battle of Gettysburg, the *Messenger* still held out a bright hope for the South as a redeemer nation: "Our fully aroused feelings have given us a deep insight into our spiritual nature, and we there behold the elements of that higher civilization which shall finally vindicate our descent from a race that destiny has appointed to hold the sceptre among men."

In January 1864, the *Messenger* changed hands for the last time. In his inaugural comment, the new editor, Frank H. Alfriend, pressed a home truth: the low status accorded literary men had meant that much of what had been written about southern institutions had been perpetrated by unsympathetic outsiders. A professional class had to be honored: "Like other people, literary men must be supported in order to live—let the Southern people then, for the first time in their history, give a practical expression of the conviction that literary men may be useful and not merely ornamental members of society." But the hour was too late. The *Messenger's* voice had grown old and hoarse; with the July 1864 issue it expired forever. Less than a year later, northern troops—those despised "Saxons"—swarmed over the city that had been its birthplace.

The wavering fortunes and the ultimate death of the *Messenger,* like those of the many literary journals which had fallen before it did, may be attributed to a number of causes, many of which it had itself identified. In the first place, the majority of these journals remained parochial—small affairs which were not widely read outside their immediate range. None could really claim to speak for "the South." A sprawling territory and a rural population militated against any widespread clamor for a literary organ. Swayed by the South's undeniable talents in political debate and forensics, these journals deluded themselves into believing that belletristic genius was naturally present in their people. But professional writing requires a professional spirit—and public support. The code of the elite—the notion that polite letters were but by-products of idle afternoons—left the would-be professional in despair.

More importantly, the self-imposed cultural isolation of the South in these decades simply stopped the clock; the literary models at the beginning of the period were still stubbornly embraced at its close. In such an atmosphere imitation was inevitable, experimentation unlikely, and progress impossible. For all the South's sneers at "Saxon" materialism, it was the North which was creating the first great period of American literature.

THREE

The Southern Romance: The Matter of Virginia

READERS of magazines like the *Messenger* were often treated to nostalgic glimpses of olden times; the sight of the ruined church tower at Jamestown was good for any number of columns of sentimental posturing, and the fate of the red man, now that he was no longer any real peril, was a natural theme for weepy elegiac verse. But the full-scale revivification of southern history was the province of the writers of long romances, and they quickly developed a gratifying thesis: a noble past prefigured a glorious future. William Gilmore Simms would make a hyperbolic claim for the genre in his preface to *The Yemassee:* "The modern Romance is the substitute which the people of the present day offer for the ancient epic." All of American history had seemed pretty barren soil in which to plant the flower of romance; Nathaniel Hawthorne was still bemoaning its commonplaceness in the 1850s. But Simms was entirely serious in discerning "epic" possibilities in native materials. In the few years since Scott had initiated the vogue for historical romance with *Waverley* (1814), northern writers like Washington Irving and James Fenimore Cooper and a host of minor imitators had been gratifying literary nationalists with an outpouring of vividly imagined scenes from colonial times through the Revolution. Now it was the turn of the South to give its own special embellishment to the country's annals.

From the 1830s through the 1850s, the romance—that fictional form which is characterized by the free exercise of the imagination rather than by strict fidelity to actuality—was the most ambitious of the South's literary endeavors. This body of fiction, it should be said at once, offers few purely esthetic pleasures, and it is generally arduous going for the modern reader. Yet these prolonged tales have a special usefulness in the study of the growth of the mind of the South. Collectively they form a psychological record of the developing conviction of separatism; they are more revelatory of inner hopes and fears than their creators could have known. In helping to give form to the southerner's sense of personal and regional identity, they performed a real social function. The legend—the myth—of the uniqueness and ordained role of the plantation South was to be relatively short in the making. But its pervasiveness and its durability in the American, even the foreign, consciousness have been extraordinary.

It was fitting, perhaps inevitable, that Virginia writers should take the lead in developing a fiction which would reorder the past in the service of the present, for here the roots were deepest. Among the earliest to contribute was William Wirt (1772–1834), Maryland-born but a Virginia lawyer by adoption. In 1803 he published *The Letters of the British Spy,* a series of essays cast in the form of the "foreign traveler" genre. Narrative interest is minimal, but these "letters," which purport to be from a young Englishman of rank to a friend in the English Parliament, reveal Wirt's conviction that Virginia had been preeminent in the nation's history. As a child of the eighteenth century, he expressed some doubt that the rising generation could live up to the monumental figures of the Revolutionary age. But as a budding romanticist and zealous patriot, Wirt tended toward the celebratory rather than the satirical mode. He paraded before his readers emotionally charged scenes which he intended to inspire prideful response. The most notable, and the most rhetorically embellished, of these inspirational outbursts are those which deal with the initial confrontation of Englishman and Indian at Jamestown. Wirt's "Spy" spends a good bit of time in the area; in one passage, as he travels over the lands where the young Pocahontas had frolicked, he cannot "help recalling the principal features of her history; and heaving a sigh of mingled pity and veneration to her memory." He goes on, rather breathlessly:

Good Heaven! What an eventful life was hers! To speak of nothing else, the arrival of the English in her father's dominions must have appeared (as indeed it turned out to be) a most portentous phenomenon. It is not easy for us to conceive the amazement and consternation which must have filled her mind and that of her nation at the first appearance of our countrymen. Their great ship, with all her sails spread, advancing in solemn majesty to the shore; their complexion; their dress; their language; their domestic animals; their cargo of new and glittering wealth; and then the thunder and irresistible force of their artillery; the distant country announced by them, far beyond the great water, of which the oldest Indian had never heard, or thought, or dreamed—all this was so new, so wonderful, so tremendous, that I do seriously suppose, the personal descent of an army of Milton's celestial angels, robed in light, sporting in the bright beams of the sun and redoubling their splendour, making divine harmony with their golden harps, or playing with the bolt and chasing the rapid lightning of heaven, would excite not more astonishment in Great Britain than did the debarkation of the English among the aborigines of Virginia.

Wirt's effusive words turn the pencil strokes of historical fact into a huge allegorical canvas; the moment is made epic. But the "Spy" knows the subsequent cost to the Indians themselves, and he drops the appropriate tear over their sufferings. He suggests that Virginians might partially redress these grievances by instituting an annual festival to honor the aid given by Pocahontas, the first American heroine:

Unfortunate princess! She deserved a happier fate! But I am consoled by these reflections: first, that she sees her descendants among the most respectable families in Virginia; and that they are not only superior to the false shame of disavowing her as their ancestor; but that they pride themselves, and with reason too, on the honour of their descent; secondly, that she herself has gone to a country, where she finds her noble wishes realized; where the distinction of colour is no more; but where, indeed, it is perfectly immaterial "what complexion an Indian or an African sun may have burned" on the pilgrim.

The "Spy" is scarcely less dithyrambic when, switching the point of view, he ruminates at the site of Jamestown itself on the portent in its founding:

Where is Smith, that pink of gallantry, that flower of chivalry? I fancy that I can see their first, slow and cautious approach to the shore; their keen and vigilant eyes piercing the forest in every direction, to detect the lurking Indian, with his tomahawk, bow and arrow. Good heavens! what an enterprise! how full of the most fearful perils! and yet how entirely profitless to the daring men who personally undertook and achieved it! . . .

It is curious to reflect, what a nation, in the course of two hundred years, has sprung up and flourished from the feeble, sickly germ which was planted here! Little did our short-sighted court suspect the conflict which she was preparing for herself; the convulsive throe by which her infant colony would in a few years burst from her, and start into a political importance that would astonish the earth.

It is no wonder that Wirt's book proved widely popular; he saw the colonial history of Virginia as providential and he adumbrated a theme which would be thundered by writers yet to come: the manifest destiny of the region. He also caught the mood of a transitional period when literary taste was beginning to reject dry and rationalistic prose in favor of the more personal and emotional. What his "letters" lacked was a strong story line. It was an auspicious beginning, but some two decades would elapse before Virginia writers would develop a sustained fictional mode. By then the models were more plentiful.

The "Matter of Virginia," which Wirt was one of the earliest to seize upon, was taken up by an authentic English observer, John Davis, who published in 1805 a long novel on the Smith-Pocahontas legend, *The First Settlers of Virginia.* In this tale and in several other writings, Davis sketched a recognizable locale, and he may well deserve the title of father of the Virginia novel. But 1824 really marks the start of a continuing tradition. Of two works issued in that year, the anonymous *Tales of an American Landlord,* with a frame story set in the 1790s, is a somewhat jumbled gathering of a number of stories; George Tucker's *The Valley of Shenandoah,* on the other hand, is a full-blown performance.

Like Wirt, Tucker (1775–1861) was neither a Virginian born nor a born novelist. A native of Bermuda, he immigrated at the age of twenty and attended the College of William and Mary. He was to have a long and uneven career in the law and politics, but with Jefferson's approval he was granted life tenure of the professorship of moral philosophy in the University of Virginia. In later years he was known mostly for studies of American history and political economy; his modest creative talents were to be exhibited in his Valley romance and in a satire in the Swiftian mode, *A Voyage to the Moon* (1827).

The Valley of Shenandoah is a rather tedious two-decker, but it is not without its surprises. These do not include its plot, which is a mélange of generic types currently popular in England and America, especially sentimental-domestic fiction and the tale of seduction. Tucker had written to a friend that he hoped his book would win him the fame and fortune which Cooper was enjoying, but it drew little notice and fewer dollars. The failure was not entirely unmerited. Tucker had a sharp eye for the state in which he matured and a serviceable if old-fashioned style; he simply would not venture away from tired story lines.

Because the book reveals so much about what Tucker thought would draw an audience, its narrative deserves brief summation. Set in 1796, it opens as young Edward Grayson, son of a Revolutionary War hero, returns to an estate at the northern end of the Shenandoah Valley in the hope of recouping the family fortunes, now at low ebb because of his late father's improvident benevolence. With him comes a fellow student at William and Mary, a New Yorker named James Gildon, who had been sent south by his merchant father to keep him from wedding an undesirable— because impecunious—city belle. Tucker had a chance to be original in contrasting the newer Valley settlements where Edward's mother and sister are now residing with the old Tidewater culture in which the family had originated. Unhappily, though, he allowed the story of the bankruptcy of this proud clan to become tangled in a melodramatic complication which weakens his social criticism. This steamy part of the tale turns upon the love affairs of the two young men. Grayson is smitten with Matilda Fawkner, daughter of the owner of a nearby estate; their union is being blocked by Matilda's mother, who takes a dim view of the Graysons' sinking fortunes. Gildon, who, despite a sharp tongue, is first presented rather sympathetically, turns out to be a traitorous seducer; his victim is Grayson's sister, the pallid Louisa, whose ingrained virtue proves an ineffectual barrier against the strategems of the sophisticated northerner. Before Gildon is aware of the biological consequences of his conquest (Tucker is so circumspect that the reader is similarly kept in the dark), he returns to New York, ostensibly to win his father's consent to marriage with Louisa; but he soon turns his attentions to his first love, now an heiress. Edward, finally learning of his friend's treachery, follows him to New York and attacks him on the street; in the ensuing scuffle Gildon stabs Grayson to death. The novel ends with the tying up of this lurid plot: Gildon's low character becomes public knowledge and he dies a sot; Grayson's love, Matilda, enters a Catholic convent; Louisa dies after a long illness; and old Mrs. Grayson lives on to become the Lady Bountiful of the neighborhood.

All this is tedious stuff, though it is a sort of index of contemporary popular taste. For us *The Valley of Shenandoah* remains of value only in its freezing a moment in Virginia history before defense of slavery turned the plantation romance into a more radically self-serving document. The story, it is true, makes a rather simplistic contrast between Yankee and southerner, between the eye-on-the-main-chance Gildon and the handsome, honor-proud Grayson. But Tucker's general view of Virginia society is anything but simple-minded. He comments accurately on the wasteful habits of the gentry; he deplores the decay of the old Tidewater; and he records the conflicts accompanying the growth of the western settlements. He even breaks the narrative to allow Grayson a considerable disquisition on the new "foreign" intrusion of Scotch-Irish and Germans, who, says Grayson, "will have some effect in forming the compound that is hereafter to make our national character."

Grayson's rather elitist tone in his survey of ethnic traits gives his auditor, Gildon, the chance for a query about Edward's own self-image: " 'Don't you feel, Edward, when riding over these vast domains of yours, something like a feudal Baron?' " Grayson recognizes that Gildon is casting him in the role of southern despot, so he carefully outlines the woes of the slaveholder: " 'We, of the present generation, find domestic slavery established among us, and the evil, for I freely admit it to be an evil, both moral and political, admits of no remedy that is not worse than the disease. No thinking man supposes that we could emancipate them, and safely let them remain in the country.' " Schemes for transportation or resettlement of slaves in Africa he holds to be impractical, and he outlines the problem as many Virginians would have seen it in the 1820s:

"In this choice of difficulties what are we to do? What can we do, but to select the least formidable? and since we cannot confer on them, or restore to them (if you will) some of those rights which we ourselves so highly prize, without endangering not only these, but every other we possess, we must even set down contented, and endeavour to *mitigate* a disease which admits of *no cure*. Because we do not indulge in idle declamation about the injurious consequences of domestic slavery, yet do not infer that our politicians are not insensible to them. The theme is an ungrateful one—like any other natural defect or misfortune which is incurable. We are fully aware of its disadvantages—that it checks the growth of our wealth—is repugnant to its justice—inconsistent with its principles—injurious to its morals—and dangerous to its peace. Yet after giving the subject the most serious and attentive consideration, and finding it admitted of no other safe remedy but what time may bring some centuries hence, they are fain to acquiesce in their inevitable destiny, and now consider all speculations on rights which cannot be enforced, but at the expense of still higher and dearer rights, either as the ebullitions of well-meaning but short-sighted enthusiasm, as sheer folly, or the hypocritical pretences of lovers of mischief."

Gildon turns to another sort of question: " 'You think, then, that considered merely with the eye of an economist, slavery is not a national evil.' " Grayson's reply epitomizes Tucker's sensitivity to the effects of the system on whites as well as blacks:

"Far from it," replied Edward. "It does operate to lessen very greatly the productive labour of a country—but not, I think, in the way it is commonly supposed. It is obviously the interest of the slave to make as little and consume as much as he can, if you attribute to him the first feelings of our nature, the love of ease and enjoyment—and this seems a sufficient cause why their labour, and skill, and care, should be less than that of freemen. . . . No; it is in the effect which slavery has on the whites, that the chief mischief is produced. It consigns this half of the population to idleness, or tends to consign them, both by making their labour less necessary, and by making it degrading. You observe that twice the number of menials are necessary to a man of small fortune here that are so to a man of large fortune with you. For none of our citizens, male or female, will perform the smallest domestic duties for themselves."

Tucker's critique of the indolence of slaveholders does not quite offset his vision of the bondage of the blacks for "some centuries," and perhaps he felt the duplicity of his presentation; for in the latter half of his story he sets up an emotionally charged scene of a slave auction. Grayson is forced by the pressure of his father's debts to sell off a number of old family servants. Such an auction would become a favorite target of the abolitionists, and later plantation novelists naturally avoided depicting it, until the clamor over *Uncle Tom's Cabin* made its actuality impossible to ignore. But Tucker is forthright. He sympathetically pictures the slaves as they are forced to mount a pine table and listen to the auctioneer broadcasting their physical characteristics before an unfeeling mob of bidders. His comment on the scene is proof that such treatment could at this period be openly discussed as a cause for Southern shame:

One not accustomed to this spectacle, is extremely shocked to see beings, of the same species with himself, set up for sale to the highest bidder, like horses or cattle; and even to those who have been accustomed to it, it is disagreeable, from their sympathy with the humbled and anxious slave. The weight of his fetters, the negro, who has been born and bred on a well regulated estate, hardly feels. . . . But when hoisted up to public sale, where every man has a right to purchase him, and he may be the property of one whom he never saw before, or of the worst man in the community, then the delusion vanishes, and he feels the bitterness of his lot, and his utter insignificance as a member of civilized society.

The emotional crosscurrents of this scene are characteristic of *The Valley of Shenandoah* as a whole. Tucker clearly was proud of his Virginia gentry and the beauties of the lands which they inhabit, yet he deplored their improvidence and hotheadedness. He called slavery inhuman and economically unsound, yet he foresaw no quick end to it. His book leaves us with the sense that there are smouldering fires in this society which are going to prove more tragic than are the events of the melodramatic tale which he actually tells. The melodrama finally can be seen as a mask placed over emotions with which he could not deal frankly.

Similar conflicting pressure in the literary portrayal of the slaveholding South can be found in the work of John Pendleton Kennedy (1795–1870). Like Tucker, Kennedy could picture a culture which he knew from his own close observation. He was born in Baltimore to an Irish immigrant father and a Virginian mother allied to an old Tidewater clan; the heritage would be reflected in the son's dual attraction to go-ahead mercantilism and the rootedness of an agrarian South. His place in southern letters rests on three works: *Swallow Barn* (1832), set on a Virginia plantation; *Horse-Shoe Robinson* (1835), an early contribution to the legendry of the South's role during the Revolution; and *Rob of the Bowl* (1838), a rather labored tale of political and religious rivalries in seventeenth-century Maryland. Of the three, the first proved to be the most significant in reflecting the image of a self-conscious South.

As a work of fiction, *Swallow Barn* broke no new ground; Kennedy's literary taste was conservative, founding itself on the work of Irving and recent British novelists. But his subject matter was relatively new, capitalizing upon the growing interest in Virginia's past. He knew the state well from his frequent visits to his mother's relatives; like Tucker, he saw the possibilities in contrasting southern and northern cultures. His narrator, therefore, is made a New Yorker, who has been invited by a Virginia cousin to spend some months on a Tidewater plantation. The frame story of the foreign visitor is thus similar to that which Wirt (whose biography Kennedy would later write) had employed in *The Letters of the British Spy*. The book opens with an expository epistle describing the narrator's voyage up the James River—with expostulations over the ruins of the colonial village and the nobility of Captain John Smith—and his overland trek to Swallow Barn itself. He then introduces the inhabitants of the plantation in leisurely character sketches before getting down to the thin narrative backbone. One plot line is a rather conventional recital of a comically inept wooing; another, which deals with a feud between two families over some worthless swamp property, allows a bit more originality as Kennedy gently mocks his Virginians' delight in litigation and legal verbiage and their inordinate pride in family and place. Neither of these narratives was capable of sustained development, and in the latter half of the book Kennedy had to resort to further sketches of the plantation locale and to digressions that take the form of self-contained short stories. But the discursiveness of this section did allow Kennedy to have his northern narrator confront the base upon which the plantation world rests: chattel slavery. The problems of the system are analyzed by Swallow Barn's lord and master, and his words both echo and differ in subtle ways from those of Grayson in *The Valley of Shenandoah*. The existence of slavery is unequivocally called "theoretically and morally wrong." But immediate emancipation and schemes for transportation, unfortunately, would wreck the South's social structure and leave the blacks "in greater evils than their present bondage." Instead, the master recommends radical improvements in the slave code. More strikingly, he proposes choosing a few of the older and more trustworthy men and forming them into a "feudatory"—in effect, serfs who could work for themselves as tenant farmers. How seriously we are meant to take this scheme as "solution" is unclear in Kennedy's treatment; but the whole discussion betrays a deep unease. Behind the apparently pastoral world of Swallow Barn is a garden of evil which the South must find a way to eradicate.

Contemporary reviews record that *Swallow Barn* gratified American readers by proving that another writer besides Irving and Cooper could find humor, pathos, and story interest in the commonplaces of the countryside. But Kennedy's split heritage produced a book with deeper currents than his original readers could have appreciated. As a man who responded emotionally to his own early travels, he inclined toward portraying an "ancient," aristocratic, amiable Virginia; as a budding businessman and politician who would later choose national over sectional interest, he was concerned with exposing the dangers of pride in state, family, and plantation system which led to scorn of all that lay outside its immediate orbit. As a result of these internal pulls, a good part of *Swallow Barn* is backward-looking and "historical." It counts upon legend—including a long excursus on Captain John Smith which was cut from later editions—and loaded words like "antique" and "aristocratical" to produce an atmosphere of age, status, and solidity. Kennedy even indulges in a version of the "Cavalier myth" as he lets his New Yorker reflect: "[Virginia's] early population . . . consisted of gentlemen of good name and condition, who brought within her confines a solid fund of respectability and wealth. This race of men grew vigourous in her genial atmosphere; her cloudless skies quickened and enlivened their tempers, and, in two centuries, gradually matured the sober and thinking Englishman into that spirited, imaginative being who now inhabits the lowlands of that state."

What the modern Virginian has inherited from this English gentlemanly background Kennedy dramatizes through his characters: pride in a long family line; personal honor and bravery; love of individual liberty; belief in land-holding as the only secure basis for an enduring social system; chivalric behavior toward women; conservatism in religion and politics; participation in public affairs; dislike of outside interference, especially that of a central government; recognition of an aristocracy founded upon inherited property. This is a catalog of all that seemed good in the developed plantation world. And yet—from an opposing angle of vision— Kennedy also insists on the necessity of progressivism and argues for the continuity of social change, including an eventual end to slavery. The book satirizes the provinciality of the closed Virginia society, lets its members condemn themselves through their tirades against outside interference and internal improvements, and mocks cherished states' rights. *Swallow Barn,* then, lets us see directly into the mind of a border-state writer who could be attracted both to a vision of the uniqueness of the southern past and to the hope of a glorious national future in which the South would not be forced to take a separate road. The book has long been categorized as the "first plantation novel"; it ought to be noted that it was written by a man who had no financial stake in an agrarian system.

In Kennedy's view of the Old Dominion, as in George Tucker's, the state is viewed as a sort of ideological arena in which the issues of caste, states' rights, and slavery could be argued by men of goodwill. Both writers foresaw a very gradual elimination of the slave system; neither dreamed of armed conflict as the alternative to public debate over southern claims. No such man was Beverley Tucker, who would fire the guns of civil war as early as 1836 in a romance called *The Partisan Leader.* Tucker (1784–1851) was

schooled at William and Mary and early absorbed the states'
rights doctrines of his brilliant half-brother, John Randolph of
Roanoke. Between 1816 and 1833 he saw frontier life as a
landholder and circuit judge in Missouri; the experience gave him
a local color background for a first novel, *George Balcombe*
(1836). This tale, though praised by both Poe and Simms, is a
drearily conventional narrative which is only partially redeemed
by some genre pictures of the border territory. Its predictable
approval of slavery and its homage to the planter class, however,
in no way prepare us for *The Partisan Leader: A Tale of the Future,* probably the most spectacular piece of fire-eating secession-
ism published before the 1850s. In every aspect the book is a
curiosity. Though issued in Washington in 1836, it bore on its title
page the spurious date of 1856 and the pseudonym of Edward
William Sydney. Despite this suggestion of futuristic fantasy,
though, the book was designed by Tucker, now back home again
as a law professor at his old college, as a warning to his state that
it must oppose the presidential bid of Martin Van Buren. It is
clear that for Tucker this pro-Whig message was all; his disdain
for narrative technique is such that he introduces the presumed
protagonist in the opening pages, drops him until nearly the close,
brings in the narrator as a new character at the very end of the
book, and cuts off the story without bringing any of the plot lines
to a conclusion. But the banner of secession is paraded throughout with drum rolls and huzzas; if the plot is murky, the theme is
fairly yelled in the reader's face. The internal time of the action is
put at 1849; Van Buren is about to run for his fourth term; and
the commonwealth of Virginia is in the worst dilemma of its long
history. The lower states have already formed a southern Confederacy and peacefully left the Union—not because of the slavery
issue but because of their adamant stand against the tariff. The
North is ruled by Van Buren, pictured as an oily and crafty tyrant
who works his villainies from the sanctuary of his "mansion" in
Washington. Virginia is caught in between; having hesitated in
joining its sister states, it is now in danger of being occupied by
Van Buren's men. By the end of the book, the Virginians, under
the leadership of Colonel Douglas Trevor, a United States Army
officer who travels the route from loyalty to secession, have
launched guerrilla warfare against northern forces. In the closing

pages we learn that Trevor has become Van Buren's prisoner in Washington. What will happen to the stalwart Partisan Leader? No devotee of romance can doubt that he and his brave men will outwit the despot, but Tucker defeats such frivolous story interest by returning to his narrator, who has been compiling a history of the rebellion. Here are his concluding words: "I have been interrupted in my narrative. I have hesitated whether to give this fragment to the public, until I have leisure to complete my history. On farther reflection, I have determined to do so. Let it go forth as the first *Bulletin* of that gallant contest, in which Virginia achieved her independence; lifted the soiled banner of her sovereignty from the dust, and once more vindicated her proud motto, which graces my title page,—SIC SEMPER TYRANNIS!"

As a forecast of the actual War for Southern Independence, Tucker's narrative is not very prescient. But, curiously, it did play a part in that conflict. In 1861 it was published in New York with the seductive tag "A Key to the Disunion Conspiracy" displayed on the title page; an "explanatory introduction" counseled the reader that he would "learn from the following pages that the fratricidal contest into which our country has been led is not a thing of chance, but of deliberate design, and that it has been gradually preparing for almost thirty years." Nor was the book forgotten in the South; in 1862 a Richmond publisher reissued it as "A Novel, and an Apocalypse of the Origin and Struggles of the Southern Confederacy." Thus, with their opposing emphases, did both sides agree on the accuracy of Tucker's trumpeted message: that the successful assertion of state sovereignty would inevitably lead to disunion.

The struggle of the loyalist Virginian against the outsider was also the theme of the second novel by another son of the Old Dominion, William A. Caruthers (1802–1846). Dr. Caruthers, a physician who spent the last nine years of his short life in Georgia, began a minor career in letters in 1834, when he published *The Kentuckian in New-York*. The work had a mild success as a sentimental romance; its setting of scenes in both New York and the South, and its attack on the abuses of slavery, probably justify its also being called an early example of the "intersectional novel." Caruthers, however, struck a richer vein the next year with *The Cavaliers of Virginia*. The title is a bit misleading, since the tale is essentially a romantic fantasy woven about the figure of Nathaniel Bacon, the eponymous leader in 1676 of "Bacon's Rebellion." The plot, with its typical interweaving of elements from historical and Gothic romance, is of little consequence; what is striking is Caruthers's conception of Bacon as a champion of individual liberty. The book revels in scenes of battle as the redoubtable Nathaniel engages a host of enemies; first, a group of former Cromwellian soldiers who are staging a revolt at Jamestown; next, the Indian Confederation; and, finally, the forces of the dictatorial Governor Berkeley. Not untypically in a work of this sort, Caruthers disregards history by rewarding the hero with his lady's hand and the prospect of a happy life to come. In reality, Bacon was already married and died of disease shortly after burning Jamestown to the ground. The character of the real Bacon and the consequences of his "rebellion" are still debated by historians; but, though he did do some research, Caruthers was not bound to being scrupulous in presenting any true motivations behind his hero's actions. What he felt the myth of Virginia needed was a prototypical—a pre-Revolutionary War—defender of the rights of the Virginia colonists against enemies foreign and domestic. As a romancer, it was not difficult, though quite unhistorical, for Caruthers to portray his Bacon as both a "Cavalier" and a leader of the people.

The early days of the colony provided Caruthers with an even loftier hero and a grander theme for his third and last romance, *The Knights of the Golden Horse-Shoe,* which he subtitled *A Traditionary Tale of the Cocked Hat Gentry in the Old Dominion.* Published first as a serial in the Savannah *Magnolia* during 1841 and then in book form by an Alabama printer in 1845, the tale inevitably had less circulation than *The Cavaliers.* The fact was unfortunate for Caruthers's reputation, for here he developed a theme which would agitate southern leaders through the Civil War period: the "manifest destiny" of the South to expand into western territory. The historical fact upon which Caruthers grounded his most ambitious romance was the horseback expedition led in 1716 by the lieutenant governor of the Virginia colony, Alexander Spotswood, across the Blue Ridge into the Valley of Virginia. The primary mission, according to Spotswood's own account, was "to satisfye my Self whether it was practicable to come at the [Great]

Lakes"—that is, to see if the boundaries of Virginia could be extended westward in order to forestall the incursions of New France into the territory. The settlement of the Valley was a reasonable political, military, and economic objective; under Caruthers's treatment the rather prosaic 1716 expedition becomes a true knightly quest through constant physical trials and Indian skirmishes, until the obsessed Spotswood at last looks down from a peak upon the great valley and sees the pathway to empire. The knightly—even saintly—character of Spotswood is established early as he proclaims his objective: "I will lead an expedition over yonder blue mountains, and I will triumph over the French—the Indians, and the Devil, if he chooses to join forces with them." It takes Spotswood many pages (the romance has the usual thicket of plots) to establish his "Tramontane Order" and to get it into mountain country; but in the closing pages Caruthers rises to his theme. With a Walter Scott whoop, he transmutes the historical Spotswood's band of sixty-three riders into a gaudy chivalric pageant:

It was a gallant sight to behold that bright and joyous band of cavaliers, in their plumes and brilliant dresses and fluttering banners, not yet soiled by the dust and toil of travel, as they wound through the green vistas fresh from the hands of nature, and their prancing steeds still elastic and buoyant with high blood and breeding. It cheered the heart of the veteran warrior, their commander, to see the columns file off before him as he sat upon his horse and received their salutes. The expedition numbered in its ranks some of the most hopeful scions of the old aristocratic stock of Virginia, some, whose descendants were destined to make imperishable names in the future of their country, and many whose descendants still figure honorably in the highest trusts of the republic.

As this band of paragons nears its objective, Caruthers sets Spotswood at stage center to attest to the international importance of their sally into this wild New World Eden:

After the saddles of venison, wild turkeys and pheasants, had all disappeared, the Governor led the way to the festivities of the evening by his standing toast, as in duty bound, now altered of course by the ascension of a male Sovereign to the throne [i.e., George I]. It was varied also by the services which he supposed himself to be rendering to his royal master. Every one rose up with him, as he filled his glass and gave, "*Our new Sovereign!* may the 'Tramontane Order' push the boundaries of his empire in America to the banks of the Mississippi."

Mindful of the aspirations of his own day, Caruthers appends a footnote at this point: "The Governor was too modest by half—he ought to have said to Mexico."

A few pages later the "knights" reach the pinnacle:

What a panorama there burst upon the enraptured vision of the assembled young chivalry of Virginia! Never did the eye of mortal man rest upon a more magnificent scene! . . . For hours the old veteran chief stood on the identical spot which he first occupied, drinking in rapture from the vision which he beheld. Few words were spoken by any one, after the first exclamations of surprise and enthusiasm were over. The scene was too overpowering—the grand solitudes, the sublime stillness, gave rise to profound emotions which found no utterance. . . . There lay the valley of Virginia, that garden spot of the earth, in its first freshness and purity, as it came from the hands of its Maker. Not a white man had ever trod that virgin soil, from the beginning of the world. . . .

Governor Spotswood carried his thoughts into the future, and imagined the fine country which he beheld, peopled and glowing under the hands of the husbandman, and all his bright anticipations were more than realized. At length he turned to [a young officer], who sat near him not less entranced, and said, "They call me a visionary, but what imagination ever conjured up a vision like that?"

As history this gorgeous scene is nonsense, since it is entirely conjured up by the vision of Caruthers himself. But as a sacred moment in national myth—the point at which the questers reach the threshold of unimagined wealth and power—it has its own sort of truth. Caruthers now adds one further inspired touch, lifting this minor episode into the stuff of courtly romance. From the Valley the governor writes back to the capital, exulting over the feats of the expedition and ordering a suitably knightly accolade for his gallants: "I wish you to have a Golden Horse-Shoe made for each of them to wear upon the breast, as a distinction for meritorious services: with the motto on one side, '*Sic juvat transcendere montes*,' [Thus does he rejoice to cross the mountains] and on the other, 'The Tramontane Order.' " Caruthers did not live to see his expansionist dream fulfilled, but he did see its beginnings. When he died on August 29, 1846, the first battles of the war against Mexico had already been won.

The writers just surveyed were very amateur novelists but very professional Virginians. As practitioners of the craft of fiction, they were content to serve up what fetched audiences South and North: sentimentality, Gothic shudders, rousing adventure, patriotic proclamations of the glory of the North American scene. They shunned innovation, generally wrote a leaden prose, and peopled their plots with waxwork figures. But as Virginians, they obviously felt it a duty to announce their own pride of place in the American colonial venture. They had, of course, real justification: the settlements at Roanoke and Jamestown, the development of Tidewater culture, the notable political and military contributions to the new nation. But what they were expressing was something stronger than simple vanity. Such writers were engaged in what was fast becoming a peculiar reading of history and culture: the idea that Virginia aristocrats were the foreordained leaders in the coming destiny of America itself. As yet, a novelist like Beverley Tucker was aberrant in suggesting separatist action, in fomenting a second American revolution in which the South would break away to continue the "true America." But, by gazing back selectively over the past of Virginia and by exalting early leaders like John Smith, Bacon, and Spotswood, these authors were giving a providential meaning to their own "errand into the wilderness." Unlike the New England Puritans, whose vision was intellectually and theologically far denser, they did not cast themselves as actors in a final stage of God's redeeming plan for humanity. The course of the South's future was not yet entirely clear, but—given its past—who could doubt that it would be wonderful?

The arrogance of the Virginian was often as annoying to other southerners as it was to most northerners, yet it was inspirational. Now that the way had been set for self-glorification, there was yet another "aristocratic" region which would demand equal recognition. As early as *The Valley of Shenandoah*, George Tucker had introduced a young South Carolinian, a very foppish Mr. Belmain, whose dandified ways arouse both jealousy and contempt in

Valley society. After one exchange on the difference in social practices between the two states, the South Carolinan is taunted by a Virginian: "'You are not before us in everything, I see.'" "'Oh, sir,' said Belmain, 'we yield to the old dominion in most things'— but with an air that showed how little his opinion agreed with his words." Tucker shrewdly observed that the Virginians' claim of superiority would not go unchallenged. It would have startled him to see it go largely ignored in the work of that rising son of the low-country South, William Gilmore Simms.

FOUR

The Southern Way of Life: The 1830s and '40s

WILLIAM GILMORE SIMMS was the South's one-man literary movement. Born in Charleston in 1806, he was for several decades his region's most powerful and prolific representative in national letters; he alone, in a culture which accorded low social status to the litterateur, aspired to make himself a true professional. Though he was quite popular in both North and South, he never gained the financial independence of an Irving or a Cooper; at his death in 1870 he was a broken, bankrupt, and defeated old man. In 1865 stragglers from Sherman's army had burned his plantation, with his extensive library and art gallery; in the rising smoke he had watched his dream of an ideal southern nation die forever. But his efforts for it had been truly heroic: over eighty published books, including thirty-four works of fiction, nineteen volumes of poetry, three of drama, three anthologies, three volumes of history, two of geography, six biographies, and a number of gatherings of reviews and addresses. There were also uncollected tales, poems, reviews, and essays scattered through a shelf of northern and southern periodicals; finally, many hundreds of letters, which constitute the most complete record of the few pleasures and the myriad frustrations of the southern author.

For the modern reader, Simms's most impressive contribution to the Old South's self-image is the series of long romances which he published between 1834 and 1859. Most of his plots he based on the actual history of the lower South from its settlement to the 1850s; because of this sweep it has been convenient to classify his tales either as "colonial," "Revolutionary," or "border." He prided himself on his knowledge of the facts, and he occasionally interrupted his narrative flow to set his readers straight on knotty points; but he also freely incorporated legend and tradition in what became his grand design—his own interpretation of the forces which would in time drive his state to be the first to declare itself independent of the American Union.

During the 1830s and '40s Simms worked in all three of his main fictional categories, capitalizing on both the appeal of the past and interest in the contemporary southern frontier. As the row of his books lengthened, Simms came to see a providential pattern revealed in the historical record. His region had undergone a "heroic" period in colonial and Revolutionary years. In the postwar period it had strengthened itself through expansion into the border areas; by the time in which he was writing, it was emerging as a structured society with the assurance of perfecting itself into an absolutely stable order. Through the crowded pages which he devoted to this reading of history moved a cast which included every type which had played a vital role over some three centuries—a dramatis personae unmatched in scope by any of his contemporaries.

Simms's method of control over this material was dedication to a central organizing principle: the South as a unique social structure. What was peculiar to the South was its hierarchical system, its insistence that on a chain of being each individual had to perform a specific function. At the top of this chain stood the aristocratic order—largely the planter class of wealth and "good family." Below it ranged the diverse body of merchants, artisans, yeoman farmers, frontiersmen—those whose "blood" and education precluded their playing a leadership role. At the bottom of all these were the slaves, whose position Simms saw as inexorably fixed, and those misfits (outlaws and the like) whom society would gradually winnow out. All three groups were closely bound in a complex system of interaction. Some flexibility could be granted as a talented individual of the second order sought a rightful place somewhat higher in the scale, but Simms considered the South as moving toward a stable and self-perpetuating state.

For years Simms managed a difficult task in his fiction; he had to avoid alienating a northern audience, which he needed to survive at all as a writer, but he also desired to instill a sense of identification with region among his own southern followers. This he did chiefly by portraying his South as an order in the process of *becoming*. The Golden Age still loomed ahead; unlike some other southern apologists, Simms did not make the claim, at least in his romances, that perfection had already been achieved. It is true that, as war between the states approached, he became increasingly shrill and dogmatic in public utterances; but in the realm of his fancy he tried to portray the disparities, the tensions, and the violence out of which a more perfected society would inevitably evolve. It was a self-serving dream, and it would prove a tragically delusive one. But the achievement still deserves recognition: alone of his countrymen Simms created an imaginative whole out of the materials of the southern experience.

Simms laid the foundation for his legend of the South in 1834–1835, when he published his first three long romances. The first of these, *Guy Rivers,* was set in the Georgia gold fields; it introduced the series of contemporary border tales which would extend to several other states. *The Yemassee,* a story of Indian warfare, was the initial and most successful of the colonial romances. The third volume, *The Partisan,* was his earliest attempt to treat guerrilla warfare in the Carolinas during the Revolution; it and the six volumes on the topic which followed over the years comprise the most sustained effort by a southern writer to see in the conflict an epic theme. All of these books, which he had published by northern firms, had surprisingly wide sales for an author of his place and time; soon he was being dubbed the "Southern Cooper," partly on the strength of his Indian romance, which invited comparison with the Leatherstocking series.

The Yemassee is not Simms's most accomplished work, but it has remained the most popular, with regular reprinting into the twentieth century. Perennial interest in the red man as both bloody marauder and noble savage probably accounts for its long survival. But, in terms of Simms's overall pageant, it has more significance as a "foundation myth," an account of that period when the Carolinians won permanent possession of the land from the only other claimants. The pivotal year was 1715, when the Indians, fearing further white encroachment and incited by the Spanish in Florida, mounted a war of extermination. The uprising was real enough, though hardly as crucial as Simms makes it; it is his imagination alone that lifts it into the stuff of lofty drama.

Simms's major theme is the clash of two cultures, European against aboriginal; the triumph of the invaders will doom the Indian. But the colonials themselves will be transformed by their victory; they will be "Americanized" by their assumption of control over the land. Throughout the story Simms switches the point of view from one side to the other. The Indian position is represented by Sanutee, the Yemassee chief who had once welcomed the white men and their gifts. Only now, as the tale opens, has he come to realize that he has thereby corrupted his closely knit tribal structure. The altered condition of his society is symbolized by the degradation of his own son, Occonestoga, whose body and will have been sapped by the settlers' liquor. In an effort to redeem his leader class, Sanutee dooms the youth to expulsion from the tribe and orders that the Yemassee tattoo be cut from his living flesh. Occonestoga will then be an outcast from both worlds, a man shorn of all identity. Simms saves him from this fate by an act of high melodrama. As the ceremony of expulsion is being carried out, Sanutee's wife breaks in and fatally tomahawks her son before he loses his tribal badge. But Occonestoga is the last of the Yemassee ruling dynasty. With Sanutee's own death in the final battle with the whites, the whole nation falls.

Simms exhibits sympathy for the Indians whose ancient culture is wiped out, but he assumes no guilt for the act. Though they have a prior claim to the land, history has overtaken them; their reign as "the nation" is fated to end. But what of their future? Unlike the blacks, they cannot be turned into slaves, and they are too treacherous to be taken into society on any other footing. As one colonist, an early white supremacist, remarks: "'It is utterly impossible that the whites and Indians should ever live together and agree. The nature of things is against it, and the very difference between the two, that of colour, perceptible to our most ready sentinel, the sight, must always constitute them an inferior caste in our minds.'" The solution offered is an extreme one: "'The best thing we can do for them is to send them as far as possible from communion with our people.'" Note that their color makes them an "inferior caste"; God has marked them as he had marked the race of Ham. In this book Simms reads the Indians forever out of his developing southern society.

With the end of the Yemassee war, the colonists may now begin to develop the old hunting grounds. Town and plantation are yet to develop, but Simms manages to outline the evolving class structure. Aristocracy enters the plot in the person of Governor Craven, an Englishman of noble rank who spends much of the book in disguise in order to prowl the backcountry and assess the Indian threat. Craven is the scion of a proud old English family, and Simms obviously wants his readers to see that Virginia has no exclusive claim to patrician origins. Light-hearted in manner and comparatively racy in speech, he is the epitome of the Cavalier spirit, and he occasionally annoys some of his more sober-minded followers. But that he is *the* leader, charged with the preservation of the colony in a time of extreme peril, is never in doubt. Blue blood will tell. As he moves on his secret mission among the Indians, Craven bears the burden of a people's destiny.

The emerging middle class is represented here mostly by Indian traders, small farmers, and those who make up the militia band who finally defeat the Yemassees; they are loyal followers, but only a few are given differentiated characters. It is the slave who gets fuller attention. Craven has a black body servant named Hector, and through him Simms is able to forecast the role of the black in a settled society. In a spotlighted scene, which reveals Simms's fear of the abolitionist movement, we are shown a loving master-slave relationship. Toward the close of the tale, Craven attempts to reward Hector for having saved his life during battle: "'Yes, Hector,—you are now free. I give you your freedom, old fellow. Here is money, too, and in Charleston you shall have a house to live in for yourself.'" But the black man only pours out his fear of manumission:

"I d—n to h-ll, maussa, ef I guine to be free!" roared the adhesive black, in a tone of unrestrainable determination. "I can't loss you company. . . . 'Tis onpossible, maussa, and dere's no use for talk 'bout it. De ting ain't right: and enty I know wha' kind of ting freedom is wid black man? Ha! you make Hector free, he turn wuss nor poor buckrah—he tief out of de shop—he get drunk and lie in de ditch—den, if sick come, he roll, he toss in de wet grass of de stable. . . . No, maussa— you and Dugdale [Craven's dog] berry good company for Hector. I tank God he so good—I no want any better."

This sort of protest would become a staple in the plantation novel, but here it is anachronistic. In his allusion to shop, ditch, and stable, Hector talks exactly like the black of Simms's own day. But by 1835 Simms already knew the problem: how to present a southern viewpoint without alienating a national audience. The passage is hardly subtle, yet a contemporaneous reader would likely have found it sentimentally satisfying rather than offensively political. It is Hector who rewards his paternalistic master with true devotion.

This was the technique which Simms learned in his earliest fiction: to propagandize for the southern system by letting such scenes appear to grow naturally out of the plot development. His own authorial voice he kept low-keyed. In the books to come he would occasionally speak out more freely. But the time was not yet ripe in the 1830s and '40s to defy the critics of his beloved South openly.

Because he was concerned with establishing the necessity for a privileged leader class, Simms set the affairs of the gentry at the center of most of his plots. One of their problems, at this stage of southern history, was the borderers. From his own observations on tours across the area, Simms recognized that the sprawling frontier abounded in types whose free-wheeling spirits would conflict with the expansionist aims of the large landholders. Some of these he depicted as mere bandits—the "land pirates" who preyed upon the homesteader; other, less hostile, characters he sometimes treated in the vein of frontier humor. But he also early discovered another figure who would rise to a sort of heroic status in national legendry; this was the scout, and, like Cooper before him, Simms explored the nature of this advance guard of civilization. In Simms's scheme of things he was a "natural noble," a sort of white counterpart of the noble savage. His destiny, as Cooper saw, was ambiguous. Simms, however, assigned him a specific functional role. His frontiersmen, beginning with Mark Forrester in *Guy Rivers,* usually ride as squires to their more knightly leaders. But they are far from being mere subservient aides; with their superior knowledge of the terrain, their contempt for sham, and their physical superiority, they serve as a rein on the gentry's impetuosity and occasional pomposity. The scout and the young gentleman, then, are depicted as parts of a developing whole—the ideal southern leader. Only their close interrelationship could bring about the full development of latent capabilities. John Pendleton Kennedy, too, had observed the scout; and in the titular hero of his Revolutionary War romance, *Horse-Shoe Robinson,* he had treated him as an exemplar of the spirit of rebellion against unfairly imposed authority. But neither Simms nor Kennedy fully captured the poignancy inherent in the figure of Cooper's Natty Bumppo, the prototype of the anarchic individualist fated to vanish with the westward advance of civilized society—but not without some loss to the national character.

These were serious themes involving the meaning of progress itself. Cooper, Kennedy, and Simms were all capable of portraying backcountry types in a comic vein, but theirs was not fundamentally a comic vision. It remained for the so-called "Old Southwestern humorists" to exploit the incongruities of the frontier people in the service of what they considered pure fun. These authors formed no school, and some were not southern by birth; they were lawyers, newspapermen, or others whose professions led them to journey in the raw lands. Their territory was vast and largely new to American letters: Missouri, Arkansas, Louisiana on the west, the Cotton Belt to the south, Tennessee to the north. Much of the material which they collected was already old in the oral tradition, but their motivation was not that of the later folklorist. Their interest was in "good story," often no more than an extended practical joke, and they quickly evolved a serviceable literary form. In what became the classic frontier yarn, an outsider, identifiable as superior in class and education, sets up the scene and brings on his characters; the country people then erupt, speaking in broad dialect; and the narrator closes the frame with a brief commentary which returns us to standard English and sanity. Subject matter was generally rough, earthy, and predominantly masculine: fights, sports and games, dancing and frolics, drinking bouts, con-men's tricks, the travails of doctors and lawyers confronting these untutored children of nature. The recorders of such scenes had few artistic pretensions, and they often employed pseudonyms as a mark of their diffidence. But their skills in rendering scene and character were frequently quite sharp; precisely because they looked upon themselves as amateurs they avoided the sentimentality and highfalutin diction of most contemporary fiction. They were early local colorists, protorealists; they discovered and worked the materials which Mark Twain would turn into high art.

The newspaper was the preferred medium for the brief humorous frontier narrative. Both city and country papers throughout the South regularly carried them, but it was a New York periodical, *The Spirit of the Times,* that became their principal outlet. Founded in 1831 by William T. Porter in imitation of an English sporting magazine, the *Spirit* circulated hundreds of anecdotes and tales, some reprinted from other papers, many directly contributed as Porter built up his own stable of writers. Their popularity remained so great that Porter issued two anthologies in 1845 and 1846; the first of these, *The Big Bear of Arkansas,* contained in the title story (by T. B. Thorpe) settings and themes which anticipated works by Melville and Faulkner. Porter encouraged contributions from every section of the country, and in 1846 he boasted that in one issue he had printed nearly seven pages of original matter from the pens of thirty-three correspondents. It has been estimated that the *Spirit* reached a peak circulation of over 40,000, an astonishing print run for the period.

It was also in a newspaper that the sketches of one of the most talented of southern humorists, Augustus Baldwin Longstreet, first gained an audience. A strong states' rights man and defender of slavery, Longstreet purchased a Georgia paper to which he contributed both editorials expounding his political philosophy and tales drawn from a large personal collection of frontier lore. Gathered under the title *Georgia Scenes* (1835), these sketches were the first to depict the "cracker" in all his eccentricities. The book drew the attention of Poe, who hailed Longstreet in the *Southern Literary Messenger* for his "penetrating understanding of character in general, and of Southern character in particular." The "scenes" are just that: accounts of fights, dances, a horse-swap, a gander-pulling, a militia company drill, a fox hunt, a shooting match, and other amusements and occupations of the class. A common thread is violence; unity is gained by the viewpoint of the narrator, who appears both attracted to and repelled by the strong material with which he is dealing.

Typical of this ambivalence is the first piece in the collection, "Georgia Theatrics." The sketch opens with the narrator setting the scene in a rather lofty tone: "If my memory fail me not, the 10th of June, 1809 found me, at about 11 o'clock in the forenoon, ascending a long and gentle slope in what was called 'The Dark Corner' of Lincoln [County]. I believe it took its name from the moral darkness which reigned over that portion of the county at the time of which I am speaking. If in this point of view it was but a shade darker than the rest of the county, it was inconceivably dark." The narrator hastily adds that he is not talking about the *present* county, from which, he says, he could adduce "instances of the most numerous and wonderful transitions, from vice and folly to virtue and holiness, which have ever, perhaps, been witnessed since the days of apostolic ministry." No, it was at an earlier time that this scene occurred: as he continued his walk he heard from beneath a thick undergrowth "loud, profane, and boisterous voices," threatening a fight. As he hurried near the place of tempestuous struggle, there came a cry "in the accent of keenest torture": " 'Enough! My eye's out!' " Now comes the comic turn: the narrator discovers that *all* the voices and sounds have issued from just one youth, who tauntingly tells him that he was " 'jist seein' how I could 'a' *fout*.' " Chagrined, he confesses, "All that I had heard and seen was nothing more nor less than a Lincoln rehearsal." We are meant to laugh at the gullibility of the storyteller; but, characteristically, Longstreet has him add a final paragraph which, by revealing the inner truth of the playacting, unsettles our own judgment of the incident: "I went to the ground from which [the boy] had risen, and there were the prints of his two thumbs, plunged up to the balls in the mellow earth, about the distance of a man's eyes apart; and the ground around was broken up as if two stags had been engaged upon it."

Longstreet did not feature any one character throughout his "scenes." In this he differed from most of his fellow humorists, who created prototypical figures of some that was good and much that was nasty in the frontier breed. One of the earliest was a real man. Davy Crockett had emerged from the Tennessee mountains in the 1830s and had made himself the hero of his *Narrative of the Life of David Crockett* (1834). After his death at the Alamo in 1836, writers of comic almanacs for some two decades made him the central figure in a series of tall tales. Crockett lived on in national legend as an epitome of the wild spirit of the frontier. The "whoop" supplied him by one of the exploiters of his fictitious character is often quoted, for it exemplifies his fabulous nature: "I'm that same David Crockett, fresh from the backwoods, half-horse, half-alligator, a little touched with the snapping turtle; can wade the Mississippi, leap the Ohio, ride upon a streak of lightning, and slip without a scratch down a honey locust; can whip my weight in wild-cats."

Crockett was metamorphosed into a frontier demigod. More earthly characters were the confidence-men and sham military heroes who regaled thousands of readers with their crude antics. One of the most popular was Captain Simon Suggs, the invention of Johnson J. Hooper, an Alabama newspaperman who contributed to *The Spirit of the Times*, Suggs's motto defines his character: "It is good to be shifty in a new country." Completely without principle and accomplished in deceit, Suggs gulls the gullible without fear and certainly without favor. Elected to the captaincy of a militia company, he leads a band as short on valor as on discipline. Though he speaks an outlandish dialect, he is clever enough to be able to impersonate such types as a state legislator, a Kentucky drover, and a well-to-do slave-buyer. Suggs is far nastier than a similar military buffoon, Major Jones, created by the Georgia editor William T. Thompson. Suggs's appeal appears to lie in Hooper's shrewd blending of several despicable types: the con-man, the militarist, and the politician; at the book's close Suggs is entering the race for county sheriff. Hooper puts his unsavory adventures at arm's length by enclosing them in the frame of a "biography." But the underlying meanness is not entirely contained by the ironic tone of his progenitor's prose.

In many ways the most sharply drawn of these backcountry rogues is Sut Lovingood, the hero of a number of yarns by George Washington Harris, who chose the mountain country around Knoxville, Tennessee, for his terrain. The character of this self-styled "nat'ral born durn'd fool" has appealed to later American writers from Mark Twain to William Faulkner. Many readers have found in Sut a prototype of Huckleberry Finn. Certainly both detest hypocrisy and both suffer from the squalid societies in which they roam; yet Sut displays a contempt for a far wider range of humanity. Not surprisingly, since he speaks for his region as well as himself, Sut despises circuit-riders, law officers, politicians, dandies, and even himself, His targets are many but his weapon is single: the practical joke. Recent critics have pointed out that, although Harris conventionally assumes the voice of the detached gentlemanly narrator, there is still a bond between the author and his Sut. For Harris, a strong proslavery man living in Unionist East Tennessee, was often at odds with his neighbors; Sut was a convenient mouthpiece for ideas which he could not voice in his own person.

The last major humorous book to come out of the Old Southwest was Joseph Glover Baldwin's *The Flush Times of Alabama and Mississippi* (1853). A native Virginian with some legal training, Baldwin set out in 1836 to try his luck among the prospering and notoriously litigious settlers of the lower South. The record of his stay there is very much a Virginian's—and a lawyer's—book; it relies far more on the character sketch than the wild frontier tale. His loyalty to his birthplace was such that he first sent his sketches back to be printed in the *Southern Literary Messenger* and not some local newspaper. In the chapter called "How the Times Served the Virginians," he devoted several pages to his reminiscences of the Old Dominion before turning to the rowdy society which his proud Virginia émigrés found: "The condition of society may be imagined:—vulgarity—ignorance—fussy and arrogant pretension— unmitigated rowdyism—bullying insolence, if they did not rule the hour, *seemed* to wield unchecked dominion. The workings of these choice spirits were patent upon the face of society; and the modest, unobtrusive, retiring men of worth and character (for there were many, perhaps a large majority of such) were almost lost sight of in the hurly-burly of those strange and shifting scenes."

In tribute to his predecessor, Hooper, Baldwin named his representative southwesterner Simon Suggs, Jr. Junior is no improvement over the old man. Baldwin takes a more lofty, more "literary" view of the frontier than did most of his contemporaries; his satire emphasizes the gulf between the cultural stability of Virginia and the social chaos of a get-rich-quick society. What can the future of the country be like, if it produces such a low species of humanity? His tradition-bound Virginian is at a loss in this new land: "All the habits of his life, his taste, his associations, his education—every thing—the trustingness of his disposition—his want of business qualifications—his sanguine temper—all that was Virginian in him, made him the prey, if not of imposture, at least of unfortunate speculations. Where the keenest jockey often was bit, what chance had *he?*"

Baldwin's question reveals the basic discomfort, sometimes the ill-concealed fear, of these creators of humorous fictions set in the frontier. They saw that their material had the incongruity which produced a comic effect, they often rejoiced in the wild antics of the characters they observed—and they had a very salable product. But, as modern critics have noticed, their writing frequently betrays their horror that the great unwashed might inherit this nation. Usually conservatives themselves, anti-Jacksonian in politics, inheritors of the concept of a gentry and a plebs, they attempted to contain the violence they witnessed by various strategies: by a cool, distancing frame device and by converting fundamental viciousness into play—into a comic spectacle at which they, in all their social and ethical superiority, could laugh. Yet the laugh was sometimes hollow. Independence of mind and behavior they saw as an inheritance from those who had had to fight a war to win it; the border people were levellers who simply took equality for granted. It took some emotional adjustment for these writers to exploit these free-wheeling characters without acknowledging the implicit draining away of their own superiority as social leaders. In having their fun and fearing it too, they also found that it was "good to be shifty in a new country."

FIVE

On the Eve of War: The Crucial Decade

THE DEMAND for the preservation of southern institutions was the dominant theme in regional oratory and literature during the last decade before the Civil War. Voices grew edgier, more defiant; to the North's boast of industrial might, the chant came back: "Cotton is King." Deeds, too, were more daring; attempts were made to take over Cuba and other Latin territories, in the hope of extending a slave empire. In the political arena the goal of a permanent accommodation between the two sections crumbled. It took but a decade to move from the Compromise of 1850, in which the North accepted the South's demand for a stricter fugitive slave law, to South Carolina's act of secession. Now the house was indeed fatally divided against itself.

The South's strongest voices in these years were still public and political; from national legislative halls to rural stumps oratory was the one verbal skill in which no deference had to be paid to the North. But polite letters—not so polite as they had once been—also became a field of battle. In the wrangle which followed the publication of Harriet Beecher Stowe's *Uncle Tom's Cabin* in 1852, two myths about the South collided head-on.

As the South's leading literary exponent of regional uniqueness, William Gilmore Simms turned his pen into a lance during the fiery fifties. His works of fiction were still noninflammatory; his purse still needed those northern royalties. But in his private letters his tone was growing more defiant. "I have long since regarded the separation as a now inevitable necessity," he wrote to Beverley Tucker as early as January 1850; and the author of *The Partisan Leader* could only have been gratified at the expression of such secessionist sentiment. Such ideas were safe enough among his own circle; their fraternal agreement apparently blinded him to the fact that outsiders would find in their talk evidence of a treasonable conspiracy. For, during a northern lecture tour, he made the greatest blunder in his career by speaking openly of southern superiority.

In recent years he had supplemented his income by public appearances, and in the spring of 1856 he inquired of northern literary friends if a swing through the region might prove profitable. Assured that he would be welcomed, Simms began his scheduled circuit in Buffalo on November 11, 1856. His subject —"South Carolina in the Revolution"—was one which he had calculated would draw readers of his romances and his ego was gratified when he stepped onto the stage to find an audience of some twelve hundred. It is plain that he originally intended no more than a lecture to northern historians on their neglect of his state's role during the war for independence. But more recent history made Simms change his tone. Just a few months earlier Senator Charles Sumner of Massachusetts, in the course of a speech during the Kansas debate, had made disparaging remarks about South Carolina and its then senator, Andrew Pickens Butler. Two days later, Butler's nephew, Representative Preston Smith Brooks, walked into the Senate chamber and severely beat Sumner with a cane. To Simms the incident symbolized all the past clashes between the North and his place of birth, and it was uppermost in his mind as he began his speech. From opening sentence to overheated peroration, he turned every phrase in praise of South Carolina's past into a vicious thrust at New England's present. In his final sentence he seems to have sensed that he had been too provocative: "Forgive me, my friends, if I have spoken warmly; but you would not, surely, have me speak coldly in the assertion of a Mother's honour!" His audience was not appeased. They had paid to hear a literary man speak on the national epic, and they had been given a piece of southern fire-eating. After two more appearances, Simms was being repaid in kind in newspaper reviews; not a little surprised at their vicious tone, he cancelled the rest of the tour. The North was more determined to work its will than he had supposed. Now the message was clear. By late 1857 he was advising a friend, "Let all your game lie in the constant recognition & assertion of a *Southern Nationality!*"

Southern nationality had been emerging as the grand theme of the seven-volume series on the Revolution in the lower colonies which Simms brought to completion in 1856. Their composition had covered most of his career: *The Partisan* and *Mellichampe* had appeared in the mid-1830s; *The Scout* was published in 1841; but the final four were all products of the 1850s: *Katharine Walton* (1851), *Woodcraft* (1852), *The Forayers* (1855), and *Eutaw* (1856). The first three books had developed a key Simmsian principle: that the interaction between hot-headed leader and commonsensical scout would contribute to a perfected patrician class. In the last four volumes Simms fully exploited an idea which earlier had been only implicit: that the partisan cause during the Revolution was a forecast of and a model for a freedom movement among present-day South Carolinians.

The earliest of the four, *Katharine Walton*, concentrates on divided loyalties, as British soldiery and their local allies clash with Carolinian partisan patriots. One theme dominates all the action: fidelity to the homeland takes precedence over all other claims. One British officer is even made to concede that England has erred in trying to force obedience upon the colonists. "'The true loyalty,'" he remarks, "'is to the soil or rather to the race. I am persuaded that one is never more safe in his principles than when he takes side with his kindred.'"

In his preface Simms preens himself on his own steadfastness in building up sectional legendry. When his volumes were first published, he boasts, they were "discoveries to our people. . . . no one dreamed of the abundance of our possessions of this sort— that a scene or story, picture or statue, had been wrought out of the crude masses which lay buried in our soil. . . . *Now,* South Carolina is regarded as a very storehouse for romance. She has furnished more materials for the use of art and fiction, than half the States in the Union."

Woodcraft, the next installment in the Revolutionary saga, was begun in the atmosphere of hardening southern reaction to outside attacks on slavery—especially that blockbuster of a book, *Uncle Tom's Cabin.* It was predictable that Simms would join the outcry over the decade's most provocative exposé; but he took an unexpectedly oblique course. Instead of responding in kind with an attack on northern wage slavery, Simms chose to present a panorama of what he conceived the southern system ideally to be. There can be no doubt that such was his intent; in a letter to a good friend, he pronounced his new romance "probably as good an answer to Mrs. Stowe as has been published."

Although *Woodcraft* is the fifth romance in order of appearance it is in terms of the chronology of the Revolutionary War the final chapter, the story of the return to a ravaged homeland. Cleverly, Simms set at the center of his plot Captain Porgy, the Falstaffian but still patrician partisan leader who had proved popular in earlier volumes. As the action opens, the defeated British are evacuating Charleston and trying to salvage what plunder they can—especially slaves, whom they have been shipping off to the West Indies. The Widow Eveleigh, an old friend of Porgy's, is on to this game; confronting the British commander she proves that a scheduled shipment contains blacks belonging to her and to Porgy. She forces their release, but the Tory M'Kewn, who has stolen the slaves, plans revenge by attacking the widow's party as she returns to her backwoods home.

Simms now weaves in the second strand of this first portion of the book. Porgy is on the road to his war-ruined plantation with a few ragged followers. They all feel a letdown after their daring adventures and hold little hope for a secure future. But their dark mood is dispelled as they spot the attempt by M'Kewn's men to hold up Widow Eveleigh. The skirmishing and bloodshed which follow take us back to the spirit of the earlier romances; Simms was willing thus far to live up to his readers' expectations. Finally, the widow and her retinue are rescued; she, observing the poverty of the partisans, gives them supplies to aid their homecoming.

Restoration of the plantation way of life forms the second section of the tale. M'Kewn holds a mortgage on Porgy's property, but after much plot manipulation his claim is held worthless; as the story closes, Porgy is able to look forward to a contented future on his improving acres. His home stands at the center of the plot, and clearly Simms intends it to be a microcosm of the South's agrarian system. Like Mrs. Stowe's Shelby and St. Clair, Porgy has been improvident in managing his affairs, but he is brought to the light. Only when he rebuilds his home out of the chaos of war, with the aid of his faithful retainers, can he comprehend that he has had to reestablish his right to be a leader in the peacetime world.

Responsibility to the southern societal system is further exemplified by the slaves, who, hardly fortuitously, play much more prominent roles in *Woodcraft*. Here Simms's "answer" to Mrs. Stowe is more explicit. No black in this community, so we are shown, is ever maltreated, none unhappy or uncared for, none unwilling to share the present hard lot of the leader class. Nor are slave families torn apart by sale, an accusation which Mrs. Stowe had made touchingly effective. Instead, in this paternalistic system, affection between slave and master abounds; and several episodes, including the return home of a party who have been dodging the enemy by hiding out in the swamps, accent the joys of reunion rather than the sorrows of separation.

But the slavery issue is most directly confronted in the numerous dialogs between Porgy and his cook Tom. Their close relationship in wartime had been sketched in earlier volumes. Here it is developed as Tom returns to his normal domestic station. Personal respect, outspokenness, the concern of each for the other's physical welfare—these are the truths, Simms insists, of a slave-based community. Mrs. Stowe had intruded on her book with much preachy comment; Simms, rather prudently, chose the dramatic method of making his points. As in *The Yemassee,* a touchy point is resolved in a scene of attempted manumission. Having finally settled his affairs. Porgy offers Tom his freedom as a reward fully earned by wartime service. But Tom is just as adamant as his predecessor: "'No! no! maussa,' he cried, with a sly shake of his head, 'I kain't t'ink ob letting you off dis way. Ef *I* doesn't b'long to *you, you* b'longs to *me!* . . . and you nebber guine git *you* free paper from me long as you lib.'" Mrs. Stowe's Uncle Tom goes to glory with the marks of Legree's fatal beating upon him; but Simms's Tom, lucky to have a *southern* master, remains till his death Porgy's "cook and proprietor." This scene is disingenuous, but generally Simms was plausible in presenting the South as a responsible society, one completely misunderstood by the North. Rising to defend the planter class whose aims he shared, he produced his most coherent and cogent fiction.

In the last two volumes of the Revolutionary saga, *The Forayers* and *Eutaw*, Simms somewhat unexpectedly turned away from the most immediate issues to an almost mystical celebration of the epical days of the final battles. The historical background derives from the "raids of the dog-days"—partisan attacks on the British—and the decisive battle of Eutaw Springs. Since British power is everywhere on the wane, those who have remained loyal to the crown are having chilling second thoughts about their allegiance. As ultimate victory looms, Simms shifts his readers' attention from the British and focuses on the personalities of the colonists who have taken opposite sides during the struggle. Though the plots of these two massive books, which stretch to 1,142 pages, are developed in leisurely fashion and are extended by many minor complications, Simms keeps one theme paramount: the justification of rebellion. His Tories, usually royalist snobs, cling to the protection of a motherland across the sea; his rebels seek the chance to rule themselves and to set up a native hierarchy.

Simms most effectively dramatizes this clash through several scenes between the partisan Major Willie Sinclair and his loyalist father. Old Colonel Sinclair is a true-blue Englishman of a former day, a hero who served in the Indian wars; now, however he is compelled by age and gout to sit about on his ancestral plantation and curse the American upstarts who have had the gall to engage the king's regulars. As Simms comments, the colonel "had swayed as a superior so long, and as a natural superior, that it was not possible with him to question his own legitimacy, or to acknowledge the claims of that fungus multitude, which it needed another hundred years to raise, in any degree, to a fairly human position." The colonel is occasionally referred to as "the baron," a title which harks back to John Locke's scheme for a native aristocracy in the colony. His "nobility" thus being ancient and transmissible, he cannot acknowledge that he must keep on earning the right to remain a leader. But his son Willie, like others in the rising generation, accepts continued responsibility as the key principle of an ordered society; and he finds that he must oppose the old man on many doctrines which the Colonel thinks immutable. It is not only that Willie has taken arms against his king; he has dared to act even further against his father's code by planning to marry the daughter of a lower-class supplier to the British troops. In defending his right to choose a wife, Willie speaks the strongest defense for a natural nobility which Simms ever penned. He orates in an incredibly didactic style, but his auditors get the point:

"Caste and class properly pride themselves upon the habitual refinements of mind and moral, acquired in long periods of time. This constitutes their just claim to authority; and they rightly hold themselves aloof from associations with other classes, who do not know, and do not properly value these refinements. But there is, here and there, a natural nobility in individuals, which overrides the law, and demands recognition. There are persons to whom refinement is *native*—who are *born* nobles—delicate and just in sentiment, magnanimous in soul, generous in courage, endowed with noble talents, and devoted to noble purposes. It is the duty of an aristocracy to acknowledge all such persons, as soon as found, and take them lovingly into their embrace, and seek to do them honor; and there is a twofold wisdom in doing so, since we thus add to our own resources of society, and increase our influence upon mankind at large."

The colonel's conversion to such novel social notions is slow, but when the light dawns he approaches complete repudiation of his past. Recalling his contemptuous treatment of his son, he reflects: "'I have been harsh to Willie. . . . True, he had joined the rebel cause! But the world changes. Laws change. Nations change. There must be change among men and nations, for they are mortal. There have been revolutions enough in Britain, and who was right? The present house is not that which ruled my fathers. . . . This is a new world, and why should it not have its own dynasties: Why not a new race in authority *here*—as proper as any in Britain? . . . So be it! Let Willie choose his own master. I forgive him the rebellion.'" So far could Simms's political daring go by 1856. Indeed, the colonel's speech, with its approval of a son's right to rebel and to "choose his own master," is thoroughly subversive. And there is a glint of steel in the line: "There must be change among men and nations."

In these seven tales of the Revolution, Simms had undertaken to create an exemplary epic story for the South. From *The Partisan* through *Eutaw,* the grand movement had been from despair to hope, from military occupation to a unified region triumphant in arms. Simms had portrayed all levels of society and had linked them by one central proposition: the responsibility of each to all in establishing a lasting system. But this epic period was past; now it was time for general recognition of the South's long development since that war. It was time, in other words, for Simms's contemporary South to step onto the stage of world history as an independent society, as the only "true" America.

Just how far northerners as well as southerners were coming to accept the notion of the South as a distinct entity was to be demonstrated in the nationwide furor that followed publication of *Uncle Tom's Cabin*. The novel was the major literary phenomenon of the 1850s not only because it focused anger against slavery but also because it drew rebuttals from the northern-born as well as from those who had known no other social system. Of the significant works which sought to undercut Mrs. Stowe in 1852–1854, six were written by northerners, six by native southerners, one of whom had lived in the North for twenty years, and three others were produced by northerners who had adopted the South as a home. Expectedly, stung southerners sprang instantly to the defense of their institution; northern-oriented writers tended to proclaim their allegiance to the Union and emphasized their fear that Mrs. Stowe was dangerously widening the split between the two regions.

It should be noted at once that the full implications of Mrs. Stowe's novel have been widely misunderstood from the day of its appearance right down through James Baldwin's remark in 1949 that it was "everybody's protest novel." This is not to say that the institution of slavery is not the heart of her story; in her *Key,* Mrs. Stowe specifically listed her charges: "first, the *cruel treatment* of the slaves; second, the *separation of families;* and, third, their *want of religious instruction.*" But the novel is no simplistic abolitionist tract; it is curiously ambivalent about both master and slave. Having only minimal direct knowledge of the South, Mrs. Stowe accepted as fact both northern and southern myths about the system. In her treatment of two southern masters, Shelby and St. Clair, she conceded the major defense that slavery was basically a paternalistic institution. Moreover, as southern critics gleefully pointed out, she made the nasty Simon Legree a transplanted Yankee, who himself proclaims, " 'I'm none o' yer gentleman planters, with lily fingers, to slop round and be cheated by some old cuss of an overseer!'" No doubt she intended that readers see that it was slavery itself and not southerners whom she was castigating. Southern critics took the view that she had had to make her villain a Yankee because she had been unable to locate a vicious southern master.

As "protest novel," *Uncle Tom's Cabin* is further diluted by Mrs. Stowe's techniques and beliefs. It is strongly saturated with sure-fire sentimentality; no one, it is safe to say, ever forgets the death of little Eva. It is also highly melodramatic and relies upon stagy effects, like Eliza's hazardous crossing of the Ohio River or the "ghosts" who haunt Legree in his final delirium. It is also heavily streaked with the pietistic strain which ran through other best-selling sentimental-domestic novels of the decade, like Susan Warner's *The Wide, Wide World*. It is these elements that assured strong emotional reaction in her readers. But such readers may also have responded to a fear which Mrs. Stowe shared with the southern planter: the peril to society of a large class of freed slaves. At the very end of the novel she supplies a solution which is morally and politically evasive. Emancipated blacks are to be repatriated in Africa, where a reborn race will one day fulfill God's plan. The black nation will lead the world to redemption: "And this, O Africa, latest called of nations . . . this is to be *thy* victory; by this shalt thou reign with Christ when his kingdom shall come on earth." And she makes the ex-slave George say, "'I want a country, a nation of my own.'" Even the pious Mrs. Stowe did not welcome the idea of a black as a next-door neighbor.

One of the more striking replies to *Uncle Tom's Cabin* was penned by Caroline Lee Hentz, a transplanted northerner who, fittingly, shared a number of traits with Mrs. Stowe. Born in Massachusetts, Mrs. Hentz had followed her brilliant but eccentric French husband around much of the Deep South for many years. Like many of the women coming into the literary marketplace in the 1840s and '50s, she discovered that writing could provide much-needed family support. (Ill, impecunious, or improvident husbands have much to answer for in directly causing the overproduction of lachrymose tales in these decades.) Mrs. Hentz had a surprising success with her fiction about the South; in 1852 she produced in *Marcus Warland* one of the earliest romances by a

woman supporting its way of life. Spurred on by Mrs. Stowe's
notoriety, she rose to the height of her powers in *The Planter's
Northern Bride* (1854). That this is not the work of a southern
hothead she gently reminds us in her preface; northern-born herself, she deplores the "intolerant and fanatical spirit" which is unfairly singling out her adopted home for criticism: "We believe
that there are a host of noble, liberal minds, of warm, generous,
candid hearts, at the North, that will bear us out in our views of
Southern character, and that feel with us that our *national* honour
is tarnished, when a portion of our country is held up to public
disgrace and foreign insult." But northerners are generally ill-
informed, she argues, and in her next paragraph she takes a swipe
at Mrs. Stowe's lack of personal acquaintance with the South,
which has led to an inaccurate portrayal of the life of the slave:

When we have seen the dark and horrible pictures drawn of slavery
and exhibited to a gazing world, we have wondered if we were one of
those favoured individuals to whom the fair side of life is ever turned,
or whether we were created with a moral blindness, incapable of dis-
tinguishing its lights and shadows. One thing is certain, and if we were
on judicial oath we would repeat it, that during our residence in the
South, we have never *witnessed* one scene of cruelty or oppression,
never beheld a chain or a manacle, or the infliction of a punishment
more severe than parental authority would be justified in applying to
filial disobedience or transgression. This is not owing to our being
placed in a limited sphere of observation, for we have seen and
studied domestic, social, and plantation life, in Carolina, Alabama,
Georgia, and Florida.

Secure in her experience, Mrs. Hentz next lays into the activities
of the abolitionists: "We give it as our honest belief, that the
negroes of the South are the happiest *labouring class* on the face
of the globe. . . . The fugitives who fly to the Northern States are
no proof against the truth of this statement. They have most of
them been made disaffected by the influence of others—tempted
by promises which are seldom fulfilled. Even in the garden of
Eden, the seeds of discontent and rebellion were sown; surely we
need not wonder that they sometimes take root in the beautiful
groves of the South."

Despite her detection of the foreign serpent in the southern garden, Mrs. Hentz made a strenuous effort to give the North a fair hearing. In the first third of a very long book, she allows her southern planter, who is in the North on business, to converse with New Englanders who marshal very telling antislavery arguments. It is with the daughter of the most hardened of these abolitionists that he inevitably falls in love, and he wins her hand only when the father recognizes that to block their marriage would likely cause their deaths from broken hearts. The remainder of the book, set in an idealized but carefully detailed South, recounts the "Northern bride's" joys and trials in her new home. Some scenes are specific retorts to actions described in *Uncle Tom's Cabin,* but Mrs. Hentz plays up romance—the true love which unites a family, white and black. Her addresses to her readers become less polemical, and in her closing paragraphs she sounds the note of accommodation: "Not merely in the expectation of honour or profit have we entered the lists as a champion of the South, but from a motive which we glory in acknowledging. We love it as the home of noble, generous hearts, of ingenuous and lofty minds. We love the magnanimity and chivalry of its sons, the pure and high-toned spirit that animates its daughters." The imagery here is that which had been enshrined in thirty years of plantation novels: knightly champion, chivalric men, pure maidens. But in her final lines she turns to an apocalyptic vision. She loves the North, too, she asserts—that North "of minds exalted and refined, of hearts steadfast and true," which "needs no champion to assert its uninvaded rights." "But," she concludes, "should the burning lava of anarchy and servile war roll over the plains of the South, and bury, under its fiery waves, its social and domestic institutions, it will not suffer alone. The North and the South are branches of the same parent tree, and the lightning bolt that shivers the one, must scorch and wither the other."

In 1854 Mrs. Hentz could still see the destinies of the two regions as inexorably linked. Some six years later that hope was dead. As Simms wrote to a northern friend in November 1860; "You may rest assured of two things, not only that S. C. will secede, & be followed by other States, but that never again can the South be possibly united with New England." A month later South Carolina did indeed secede, and the vocabulary of the Old South passed into the rhetoric of the Confederacy.

When Hinton Rowan Helper published his best-selling antislavery tract, *The Impending Crisis of the South,* in 1857, he closed his diatribe with a look at "Southern literature." A North Carolinian, Helper announced in his preface that he hoped his "countrymen of the South" would discern in his analysis of the political and economic ills caused by the slave system no real disloyalty to his own region. He made his intention very clear: "It has been no part of my purpose to cast unmerited opprobrium upon slaveholders, or to display any special friendliness or sympathy for the blacks. I have considered my subject more particularly with reference to its economic aspects as regards the white—not with reference, except in a very slight degree, to its humanitarian or religious aspects." Helper was commendably forthright in exposing his own prejudice: he disliked blacks but he hated slavery as the enemy of free labor.

His views were partly shaped by the abolitionist myth that a slaveocracy totally controlled the South and that intellectual pre-eminence was simply impossible under such a system. Yet his condemnation of the achievement of southern writers has the merit of being an insider's judgment. Much of his chapter—as was his wont—is drily statistical, and he muddied his discussion by cramming under his rubric "all the activities engaged in the creation, publication, and sale of books and periodicals." But he spotted most of the underlying weaknesses and laid them out seriatim. His opening points are familiar: southerners are not a reading people and they simply won't support a periodical press. But he also touches on an increasingly tender spot: the fact that the South had to import its school texts and reference works. In a character-istic passage of slanging, Helper underscores the paradox:

Southern divines give us elaborate "Bible Arguments"; Southern statists heap treatise upon treatise through which the Federal Constitution is tortured into all monstrous shapes; Southern novelists bore us *ad infinitum* with pictures of the beatitudes of plantation life and the negro-quarters; Southern verse-wrights drone out their drowsy dactyls or grow ventri[cose] with their turgid heroes, all in defence of slavery,— priest, politician, novelist, bardling, severally ringing the changes upon "the Biblical institution," "the conservative institution," "the humaniz-ing institution," "the patriarchal institution"—and then—have their books printed on Northern paper, with Northern types, by Northern artizans, stitched, bound, and made ready for the market by Northern industry; and yet fail to see in all this, as a true philosophical mind must see, an overwhelming refutation of their miserable sophisms in behalf of a system against which humanity in all its impulses and aspirations, and civilization in all its activities and triumphs, utter their perpetual protest.

Helper now falls into capitals to propound his summary question and supply its answer: "WHAT HAS PRODUCED THIS LITERARY PAU-PERISM OF THE SOUTH? One single word, most pregnant in its terrible meanings, answers the question. That word is—SLAVERY!" And he winds up, axiomatically, "*Literature and Liberty are inseparable; the one can never have a vigorous existence without being wedded to the other.*"

The fact that great literatures have been produced in slave societies—in classical times, for example—is no real retort to Helper; his analysis has an immediate ring of plausibility. For decades historians of American literature echoed him: the Old South failed because its writers were forced to defend an indefensible institution. It was, of course, impossible for writers to ignore the presence of slavery; but it was not black slavery alone which locked them into a mental prison. What hedged them in was their sense that they had to support the *whole* "Southern way of life," from its top to its bottom layer. Such an atmosphere was not conducive to independent literary activity. When southern promoters blew the call for a native literature, the trumpet gave no uncertain sound. They did not mean a literature written *in* the South; they meant a literature *about*—and subservient to—basic southern interests.

Perhaps the greatest block to the realization of more lofty goals was the notion which they had helped to disseminate: that the South truly possessed an aristocracy whose tone would create and whose wealth would support an indigenous literary culture. But the upper class was not a leisure class, despite the widespread myth that it was. The wealthiest did indeed build splendid mansions and, like most parvenus, they filled them with imported art and furniture. Yet these great houses were often no more than a public statement of their owners' status; their architecture proclaimed that here dwelt men and women dedicated to classical ideals. But, while the gentry appreciated beauty, they cared little for the artistic temperament that had produced it. They looked on belles lettres as a grace note; they would have been repelled by a literature of ideas. Such an attitude was hardly unique to the Old South, but that its writers persisted in glorifying a structured society in which they had no ordained place is an irony which they seemed not to comprehend.

In a region in which conservatism of taste was a matter of pride, writers also remained locked into imitation of the literary models which were dominant when the South began the retreat from the rest of the nation. Their fiction—the historical romance, the Gothic and melodramatic tale, the sentimental-domestic novel —advanced very little in technique during a period of three decades. Though theater-going was a popular amusement, native dramatists contributed little of worth to the repertory. Southern poets, whom Helper accurately, if meanly, called "verse-wrights," knew their Scott, Byron, Burns, Campbell, and Moore, and they saw no reason to drop old favorites. Their lines, regularly printed in newspapers and magazines and occasionally collected in books, were, at best, competent craftsmanship. They elevated sound over sense, sensibility over intellectuality; they practiced a stylized lyricism in which it would have been bad form to sound a strictly personal note. In short, a collective conservatism of mind made experimentation and individualism not only unlikely but futile. "Correctness" was all.

It is not difficult to make this sweeping judgment of actual literary accomplishment; equally it is easy for the modern critic to point out the great body of potential material which the Old South neglected: Indian culture; an ancient oral tradition; the songs and tales of the slaves; the everyday dramas of city, plantation, and backwoods. But "realism" had not yet developed as a literary mode; celebration of the ideal and not depiction of the "actual" was what "art" was all about. And it was not just southern snobbism that kept the great mass of folk literature out of print. No right-minded critic anywhere in the country would have proclaimed that there might be more art in, say, a Negro spiritual than in the verse of a Simms. The South had imprisoned itself in the notion that literary form was as immutable as its social structure. It was not impossible for a genius to arise in such a region; it was simply impossible for him to flourish.

For all its failure to produce a significant written literature, though, the Old South had done something truly remarkable; by its close it had created a transcendent fiction. That fiction was its annunciation of a unique identity, a divinely sanctioned social order which alone could fulfill the destiny of the true America: to establish an agrarian empire which would override the soul-crushing, industrialized North. This South was to be the first really new society in the New World, an Arcadia in a moral wasteland, a nation firmly set against the currents of modern history. The concept had electrifying power, but it was about to be exposed for what it was—a fiction.

SIX

The Confederacy and
the Martyred South

Hath not the morning dawned with added light?
And shall not evening call another star
Out of the infinite regions of the night,
To mark this day in Heaven? At last, we are
A nation among nations; and the world
Shall soon behold in many a distant port
     Another flag unfurled!

THE LINES are from "Ethnogenesis," by Henry Timrod, the Charleston poet who set them down as the first Confederate Congress met in Montgomery in February 1861. The mood was exultant as the realization swept over the South: "A nation among nations." As the geologist Joseph Le Conte later recalled in his *Autobiography,* he had at first opposed the secession movement and dreaded the inevitable conflict; but, he added, "gradually a change came about—how, who can say? It was in the atmosphere; we breathed it in the air; it reverberated from heart to heart; it was like a spiritual contagion—good or bad, who could say? But the final result was enthusiastic unanimity of sentiment throughout the South." One doubts the unanimity of assent to any war, but thousands were indeed marching off under "another flag." After the initial southern military successes, William Gilmore Simms was able to crow to a New York friend, "We are resolved on Independence. We have been persecuted for 30 years & will stand it no longer—from our brethren. . . . Every battle, thus far, has resulted in a Southern Victory.—Sumter, Bethel, Bull Run, Manassas, Harpers Ferry & Missouri,—all tell the same tale. Your Generals are cashiered. Your army demoralized."

Simms's sneer at northern weakness of will betrays the fatal delusion of southern patriots; they could not fail because they were asserting fundamental political rights. Even after the war was lost, a writer in the *Southern Presbyterian Review* could still state with conviction the philosophical ground upon which the South had stood: "The thing on trial in the American Union, as Southern men thought, was *liberty*—constitutional liberty; the power of the States, the power of persons, to maintain all their constitutional rights, against all claims of power whatever; against the irresponsible constructions of the extent of its own powers by the Federal Government; against reckless and passionate majorities." Simms had earlier supplied a more mundane consideration. In a public reply to a northern correspondent who had spoken for the preservation of "the blessed Union," he retorted: "We can easily conceive the reluctance of your section to see it dissolved. The Union . . . has been the source of all your prosperity. You have, at length, destroyed it. . . . You have allowed our enemies— and I think your own—to triumph; and if you will permit me to say, *now,* your present mistake still consists in the desire, *rather to save the Union, than to do justice to the South.*"

The dissolution of the Union, welcomed though it was by such men as Simms, left the South in almost complete cultural isolation. The disruption of supply routes, especially the blockade of southern ports, dried up the flow of both northern and European publications. But local entrepreneurs now saw an unprecedented chance to rout northerners from southern library tables as well as from southern fields. As the *Southern Illustrated News* put it in 1862, readers would no longer be forced to buy "the trashy productions of itinerant Yankees . . . but will, in future, have Southern books, written by Southern gentlemen, printed on Southern type, and sold by Southern publishing houses." For a time the claim was made good; books were indeed more widely circulated and wartime magazines proliferated. But, as all commodities grew scarce in the closing years of the war, production and distribution became more difficult; few periodicals survived their infancy. Moreover, as editors had been complaining for years, southerners were a capricious people; when things got tough, they always deserted first the artists who were toiling to create pride in southern letters.

In fact, the formal literature of the wartime South was not much to take pride in. What best expressed the true feelings of beset southerners were the ballads, songs, and poems which had both folk and written circulation. Military bands and parlor pianos alike cheered hearts with songs like "The Bonnie Blue Flag," with its stirring chorus of "Hurrah! Hurrah! for Southern rights, Hurrah!" As in all wars, soldiers recalled old tunes and set new words to them, sometimes patriotic paeans to their states or military units, occasionally scurrilous reflections upon their commanders. The violence and horror of the most tremendous conflict fought upon the North American continent stirred writers on both sides to produce a sizable amount of often moving verse.

After defeat, Simms recognized that such works would be an important part of the record of the inner life of his people. In the preface to his anthology *War Poetry of the South* (1867), he could also plead that the North accept it as a contribution to the national heritage: "Though sectional in its character, and indicative of a temper and a feeling which were in conflict with nationality, yet, now that the States of the Union have been resolved into one nation, this collection is essentially as much the property of the whole as are the captured cannon which were employed against it during the progress of the late war. It belongs to the national literature, and will hereafter be regarded as constituting a proper part of it, just as legitimately to be recognized by the nation as are the rival ballads of the cavaliers and roundheads, by the English, in the great civil conflict of their country." Tactfully, Simms did not identify which people were "cavaliers" and which "roundheads."

Actually the best of southern wartime poems were those which commemorated not the triumphs of the Confederacy but its horrendous collapse. In the stunned silence of surrender, the price of it all moved the hearts of those who had so joyously greeted the birth of a nation. It was Father Abram Joseph Ryan, a militant Catholic cleric who refused to be reconciled to the Union until 1878, who most memorably echoed what he called "the unuttered feelings of the Southern people" in his hymn to "The Conquered Banner." The first stanza, despite its heavily reiterative rhyme pattern, rises to a true elegiac pitch:

Furl that Banner, for 'tis weary;
Round its staff 'tis drooping dreary;
    Furl it, fold it, it is best;
For there's not a man to wave it,
And there's not a sword to save it,
And there's no one left to lave it
In the blood which heroes gave it;
And its foes now scorn and brave it;
    Furl it, hide it—let it rest!

In the final two stanzas despondency is assuaged by Father Ryan's forecast that the deeds of the Confederacy will enter hallowed history:

Furl that Banner! True, 'tis gory,
Yet 'tis wreathed around with glory,
And 'twill live in song and story
    Though its folds are in the dust:
For its fame on brightest pages,
Penned by poets and by sages,
Shall go sounding down the ages—
Furl its folds though now we must.

Furl that Banner, softly, slowly!
Treat it gently—it is holy—
    For it droops above the dead.
Touch it not—unfold it never,
Let it droop there, furled forever,
    For its people's hopes are dead!

In such lines we hear the first chords of a tremendous new theme—the Lost Cause.

Wartime verse boosted the morale of the southern nation, but the war was to make victims of the three most talented poets of the period: Henry Timrod, Paul Hamilton Hayne, and Sidney Lanier. Timrod, who had served as a tutor on plantations in the decade before conflict began, published a collection of pallidly romantic poems in 1860. The war sharpened his tone and released the talent for occasional verse that earned him the sobriquet "Poet Laureate of the Confederacy." Ill health ended his brief service in the army; in the war years he was, variously, correspondent, reporter, and then editor of the Columbia *South Carolinian*. The sacking of the state capital by Sherman's army left Timrod destitute. Suffering from poverty and weakened by tuberculosis, he survived only until 1867. The first stanzas of his "Ode," which had been sung at the decoration of Confederate graves in a Charleston cemetery the previous year, might stand as his own epitaph:

> Sleep sweetly in your humble graves
>   Sleep, martyrs of a fallen cause;
> Though yet no marble column craves
>   The pilgrim here to pause.
>
> In seeds of laurel in the earth
>   The blossom of your fame is blown,
> And somewhere, waiting for its birth,
>   The shaft is in the stone!

Timrod's close friend, Paul Hamilton Hayne, would live some years beyond the war's end; but he, too, lost his house and possessions to northern invaders. In 1866 he settled with his small family in a shack in the pine barrens west of Augusta, Georgia; it would be his home for the last twenty years of a life of poverty, literary drudgery, and ill health. As a link between Old South and New, and as heir to Simms of what remained of a southern literary establishment, he tried to encourage new talent. His own verse, however, remained old-fashioned, just as his political sentiments went unreconstructed. And yet he kept up a surprisingly large correspondence with northern and even English writers; in literature, at least, he attempted to allay sectional prejudices. It is hard to say whether a less isolated life and a closer contact with the developing cultural life of the nation might have made a better poet of Hayne; likely, his taste for the ornate, his love of subject matter remote from everyday affairs would never have been significantly altered. In retrospect, he seems more important as a representative southern literary man than as the creator of memorable verse.

The youngest of these three poets, Sidney Lanier, published nothing until after the end of the Civil War; but, like the other two, he was wrecked physically during the war and shared in the general poverty of the postwar South. Lanier saw war at firsthand in some of the great Virginia battles; in 1864 he was captured and sent to a federal prison in Maryland. When he emerged he was afflicted with the tuberculosis that would undercut his strength during his final sixteen years of life. Lanier's first book, a novel called *Tiger-Lilies* (1867), suffered general, and not unwarranted, neglect, even though it contains inside views of his life in military prison.

Despite the undeniable achievements of his later years, Lanier scattered his talents. Early drawn to music, he became for a time first flutist in the Peabody Symphony Orchestra in Baltimore. In Baltimore, too, he achieved a second ambition—to be a literary scholar—when he was appointed lecturer in English at the recently founded Johns Hopkins University. Poetry, though, remained his chief love; and in the mid-1870s his work began to receive national recognition. "Corn," written in Georgia, was a plea for an agricultural reform that might lead to a new South, one free of the domination of a single cash crop. "The Symphony," printed in 1875, uses the imagery of music, which he saw as a universally harmonizing force, to protest the rise of commercialism. With "The Marshes of Glynn," Lanier achieved the dual goal of prosodic experimentation and revelation of his sense of the transcendental in nature—a linking of his esthetic and religious concerns. The poem has so frequently been anthologized as to blunt the original effect of an unexpected freshness and originality in a southern poet; but perhaps its musicality may still be heard in the closing lines:

> How still the plains of the waters be!
> The tide is in his ecstasy.
> The tide is at his highest height:
> And it is night.

> And now from the Vast of the Lord will the waters of sleep
> Roll in on the souls of men,
> But who will reveal to our waking ken
> The forms that swim and the shapes that creep
> Under the waters of sleep?
> And I would I could know what swimmeth below when the tide
> comes in
> On the length and the breadth of the marvellous marshes of Glynn.

The relative success of Lanier, however, only underscores the general aridity of poetry in the South from which he sprang. For all the straining to produce a theory of poetry—from Poe's "The Poetic Principle" to Lanier's ambitious *The Science of English Verse*—southerners never gave the poet the sort of homage which Longfellow had won in the North. This lack of concern for the professional, the inability to understand those who would make a separate career of verse-writing, was deadly to the growth of a southern school. Since good poetic models, from Pope through the recent Romantics, already existed, what encouragement could there be for the seeking of a personal and unique voice? Lanier's discovery of Walt Whitman as late as 1878 is revelatory of his region's cultural backwardness. Writing to a friend from whom he had borrowed the book, he remarked: "LEAVES OF GRASS was a real refreshment to me—like rude salt spray in your face—," though Lanier had to confess that his reaction was "in spite of its enormous fundamental error that a thing is good because it is natural, and in spite of the world-wide difference between my own conceptions of art and its author's." A short time later, Lanier wrote to Whitman himself, seeking to buy a copy of his volume and sounding a more appreciative note: "It is not known to me where I can find another modern song at once so large and so naive: and the time needs to be told few things so much as the absolute personality of the person, the sufficiency of the man's manhood *to* the man, which you have propounded in such strong and beautiful rhythms."

Lanier's tribute is touching evidence of his sense of provinciality. And it was also a testimonial to the accuracy of his friend Timrod, who had made one of the acutest analyses of the restraints put upon the poet in his essay "Literature in the South." Timrod opened his piece with what had become a truism: "In no country in which literature has ever flourished has an author obtained so limited an audience." The chief reason, Timrod felt, was simple sectional prejudice:

It is the settled conviction of the North that genius is indigenous there, and flourishes only in a Northern atmosphere. It is the equally firm conviction of the South that genius—literary genius, at least—is an exotic that will not flower on Southern soil. Probably the book [of a

Southern writer] is published by a Northern house. Straightway all the newspapers of the South are indignant that the author did not choose a Southern printer, and address himself more particularly to a Southern community. He heeds their criticism, and of his next book,— published by a Southern printer—such is the secret though unacknowledged prejudice against Southern authors—he finds that more than one half of a small edition remains upon his hands. Perhaps the book contains a correct and beautiful picture of our peculiar state of society. The North is inattentive or abusive, and the South unthankful, or, at most, indifferent.

Timrod now focussed his attack: "The truth is, it must be confessed, that though an educated, we are a provincial, and not a highly cultivated people. At least, there is among us a very general want of a high critical culture." Part of the South's problem, he admitted, was shared with the North—the cry earlier in the century for "Americanism" in literature. "To be an American poet, it was sufficient either in a style and measure imitated from Pope and Goldsmith, or in the more modern style and measure of Scott and Wordsworth, to describe the vast prairies of the West, the swamps and pine forests of the South, or the great lakes and broad rivers of the North. It signified nothing to these critics whether the tone, the spirit, or the style were caught from European writers or not. If a poet, in genuine Scott, or genuine Byron, compared his hero to a cougar or grisly bear—patriotically ignoring the Asiatic tiger or the African lion—the exclamation of the critic was, 'How intensely American!' "

Timrod was no supporter of more recent regionalism: "We regard the theory of Southernism in literature as a circumscription both unnecessary and unreasonable, of the privilege of genius." In a closing shot, he aimed at the local arbiters of taste who would deny personal freedom to the southern author:

After all, the chief impediment to a broad, deep, and liberal culture is her own self-complacency. With a strange inconsistency, the very persons who decry Southern literature are forever extolling Southern taste, Southern learning, and Southern civilization. There is scarcely a city of any size in the South which has not its clique of amateur critics, poets and philosophers, the regular business of whom is to demonstrate truisms, settle questions which nobody else would think of discussing,

to confirm themselves in opinions which have been picked up from the
rubbish of seventy years agone, and above all to persuade each other
that together they constitute a society not much inferior to that in
which figured Burke and Johnson, Goldsmith and Sir Joshua. All of
these being oracles, they are unwilling to acknowledge the claims of a
professional writer, lest in doing so they should disparage their own
authority. It is time that their self-complacency should be disturbed.

The critique was entirely just. But it was published in 1859 and
was an insider's plea to his own culture for greater artistic freedom.
It was the fate of the southern poet, however, that he could not
escape his time and place. Within two years after the publication
of his diatribe, Timrod gave his pen unreservedly to the defense of
this same culture. Now the quondam impugner of southern self-
complacency could see danger only in enemies from the outside—
those northern hordes who, he wrote in "Ethnogenesis," "might
with a hostile step profane our sod!"

The North-South clash which reached its military conclusion at
Appomattox could not so definitively be settled in the minds and
emotions of the reunited American people. Though Lincoln had
promised in his second inaugural address to "bind up the nation's
wounds" and to exhibit "malice toward none," the Radical Repub-
licans who took over control of the South in the decade of Reconstruction quickly abandoned Lincoln's sympathetic approach.
The once-proud southern states were divided into military dis-
tricts and placed under martial law. Thousands of white voters
were disenfranchised, while scores of ex-slaves were placed in
positions of authority. It was to be expected that white southerners would respond with Black Codes to ensure their own political
domination over Negroes and with vigilante bands like the Ku
Klux Klan to terrify them. The North had destroyed the Confederacy and left it a ruined and occupied land; it could not ex-
tirpate the southern spirit.

For now the South had its own history, quite apart from that
of the Union. It had its heroes, men far grander than those
imagined by its romancers: the knightly Lee, the saintly Jackson,
the dashing Mosby. Its sacred battlefields, soaked with the blood of
martyrs, stretched wide across the land: Bull Run, Antietam, Get-

tysburg, Chancellorsville, the Wilderness. Of the great ironies of
southern history, one of the most striking is that no great poet
arose to hymn its arms and men, no Tolstoy wove together the
story of those hellish days at Gettysburg. There were, of course,
scores of biographies, massive histories recounting the course of
the war as seen from a distinctly southern point of view. There
was the ultimate defense of the southern cause written by Jefferson
Davis, who alone of southern leaders had refused amnesty. Its
title proclaimed the grandeur he saw in his theme: *The Rise and
Fall of the Confederate Government*. But the fact remains that no
poet or novelist ever had the moral nerve to confront the meanings of the nation's greatest trauma; it remained, in the phrase of
a recent critic, "the unwritten war." Perhaps the horror of battle
was too great, the memory too recent for the literary mind to deal
with it without danger to its sanity. Perhaps, too, an emotional
resistance to recording the actual experience was linked to a refusal to shoulder the moral guilt of slavery.

Certainly some sort of psychological blockage is at the center
of the problem. But, at least in fiction, literary convention also
played a part. When a northern writer, John W. De Forest, set
down realistic battle scenes in *Miss Ravenel's Conversion from
Secession to Loyalty* (1867), he was quite aware that readers
would shrink from such gross depiction and that critics would
censure his lack of ideality. But even De Forest could not get the
whole war into the book. After he had read Tolstoy's *War and
Peace,* he wrote to William Dean Howells, "I tried, and told all
that I dared, and perhaps all that I could, but did not dare state
the extreme horror of battle and the anguish with which the
bravest soldiers struggle through it." Yet De Forest's realism was
by far the strongest in all American letters before Stephen Crane's
The Red Badge of Courage (1895). The South would never even
approach the factuality of such books.

The most typical of the southern romancers was John Esten
Cooke, who had seen the truth of combat but refused to write it
down. Cooke had published a popular tale of the colonial South,
The Virginia Comedians, as early as 1854, but he reached a
wider audience in the immediate postwar years. An active soldier,
he had served on the staff of General J. E. B. Stuart and had an

insider's view of the conflict. Beginning in 1866 with a tale called *Surry of Eagle's-Nest,* he devoted seven books to the course of the war—the first significant body of such fiction to come from either side. Son of the Old Dominion in temperament as well as birth, Cooke portrayed Lee, Stuart, and Jackson as avatars of the Cavaliers, and many a southern youth must have felt personal pride in the daring exploits through which these knightly commanders ride. He showed some skill in constructing battle scenes, but unhappily he allowed plot (and outmoded Gothic mystery at that) to overwhelm whatever historical insights he might have given his reader. The Civil War simply wasn't picturesque enough to him to sustain a whole book. True romance was always to be sought in the distant past, especially eighteenth-century Virginia, and it was romance that Cooke wanted to purvey. Quite characteristically, he told a fellow writer that he saw in modern warfare "nothing heroic or romantic or in any way calculated to appeal to the imagination." Cooke's Civil War, then, had to be reconstructed on literary models and peopled with toy soldiers; the noise and smell of the real battles he had seen were too indecorous for the taste of those who wanted heady heroics without the reek of blood.

Cooke is representative of most southern authors in the postwar decade in his refusal to acknowledge that a new voice might be needed to express the changed times. In physical bondage to their military administrators, southerners remained in what appears to be a self-imposed mental captivity. Northern books again flooded in; southern writers often found northern markets closed off to them. There were occasional exceptions. Augusta Jane Evans (Wilson), who had already had a hit with the deliriously sentimental *Beulah* in 1859, produced a nationwide best-seller in *St. Elmo* (1867), an incredible brew of melodrama, pseudo-intellectualism, and mild sex which may stand as the benchmark of the low taste of the period.

Isolation from the life of the nation again stimulated the founding of a number of local magazines, all loftily conceived and all ill financed. Sectionalism is rampant in these periodicals and some are frankly organs of Lost Cause mentality. But by the end of the Reconstruction period in 1877, the atmosphere was changing, and there seemed no pressing need for an organ to succor southern writers and broadcast their views. After a long period of vilification of their persons, their morals, their ideas—even their landscapes—southerners were about to make a triumphal entry upon the national literary scene. Many of them, of course, remained resolutely prejudiced against the North and all its ways. What was really shifting was the North's view of *them*.

SEVEN

The New South:
The Past Recaptured

THE SOUTH'S strong resistance during Reconstruction to a complete reordering of its way of life was less valorous than its wartime performance, but it was more successful. As the scars of occupation faded, its writers embarked upon a popular program of sectional justification that would have astonished the editors of scores of dead little southern journals. For northern editors were now not merely tolerating writing from the South; they were demanding it. And they not only sought it; they bought it. This episode in American literature is usually called the emergence of the "local color" school. Not only the South was involved in it, to be sure, but it was the South that ultimately proved to be richest in its materials and most prolific in its celebrants. By the 1880s the still unreconstructed must have been baffled: the South had become the most popular setting for American fiction. The wry reaction of the northern novelist Albion W. Tourgée, who had described his experiences during Reconstruction in *A Fool's Errand* (1879), is revealing. American writing, so he charged in the *Forum* magazine in 1888, has become "not only Southern in type but distinctly Confederate in sympathy. . . . A foreigner studying our current literature without knowledge of our history, and judging our civilization by our fiction, would undoubtedly conclude that the South was the seat of 'ntellectual empire in America, and the African the chief romantic element of our population."

Tourgée's sour remarks tell only part of the truth; the South was simply the chief beneficiary of a mood and a literary trend that had characterized the whole nation in the years after the close of the Civil War. In fighting for the preservation and the strengthening of the Union, the North necessarily had attacked sectionalism and campaigned for the homogenization of the American people. In constructing its giant war machine for this purpose it had stimulated industry and manufacture. The technological superiority of the Union forces was a bitter fact to the defeated Confederacy. By the 1880s some southern leaders, like Henry W. Grady, who spoke through his influential Atlanta *Constitution,* were urging that the only hope for a truly reconstructed South lay in the adoption of laissez-faire capitalism and the development of industry throughout the region. Only Grady's scarcely hidden racism— his reliance on white domination for the success of his programs— ameliorated his policy in the eyes of die-hard upholders of the old regime.

It sometimes surprises modern readers of local color fiction to observe how little the "New South" enters the picture. But this is to misunderstand its real nature. For literary taste was now strongly nostalgic. In the midst of the Gilded Age there were many who remembered what seemed to have been a less complicated, a freer, even a happier time. The war had opened a great gulf in national history; on the other shore the colors now appeared brighter, the skies more open, the people more individualistic. An age of simple elegance had vanished in an all-conquering mechanistic modernism. Where were the self-contained and pleasant little New England villages? And where now were the courtly stock who had given the South its peculiar tone?

The situation was a godsend, a boon that the defeated nation could hardly have expected. Except for the work of the humorists of the Old Southwest, northern periodicals had not been particularly receptive to tales from the South. Now northern editors were beginning to accept as fact what the South had been insisting for decades: that it was the only "romantic" society America had produced. The West—with its gunfighters, its outlaws, its cowboys and Indians—had color; what it lacked was "charm." The West was open and awe-inspiring; the South was cozy and "home."

The southern writer seized the day. No longer required to defend slavery as an *institution,* he could now, without giving offense, depict the black as the happy-go-lucky darky, still benev-

olently cared for by the white man he once had to call "master."
The Negro was considered to be the South's own special problem.
Increasingly strict Jim Crow laws were evidence of how he was
being contained in fact. In fiction, with the notable exceptions of
Cable, Harris, and Twain, this type of continued enslavement was
largely ignored. The blacks were a picturesque peasantry; their
comic speech, their superstitions, their penchant for stolen water-
melon or chicken were "realities" everyone could now laugh at—
benevolently, of course. And now that the South presented no
threat to the body politic, its quixotic attempt to establish an aristocratic empire could take on the special glamor reserved for lost
causes. Domiciled amid the ruins of its artifacts, the southern writer
could dream of the never-never land—the pillars of its plantations
grown prodigious, its ladies more classically beautiful, its men more
dashingly gallant, its gardens more lovely in the moonlight, its
field songs more melodious and soothing. Alas for the fled, alas for
the fallen!

The plantation South was the most popular version of the
myth of the past because its high-toned life now could be enjoyed
without guilt. But there were other Souths, and writers from several
sections were quick to stake out their claims. One of these areas
which was largely unexplored was the high upland and moun-
tainous Appalachian chain; though the mountaineer had long
since appeared as character in early romances and southwestern
tales, there had been little attempt to picture him in his own setting of lonely hill cabins, hardscrabble fields, dark hollows. The
authors who first penetrated this thicket were in no sense sociolo-
gists or fieldcollecting folklorists. These latter would come later
and would preserve a rich store of ballad, song, and tale—folkways that revealed much of the character of the original European
settlers. The local colorist observed some of this same material,
but he sentimentalized, softened—or, conversely, melodramatized
—the true culture of the region.

One of the most successful of these exploiters of a pocket in
time was a crippled Tennessee spinster, Mary Noailles Murfree,
who rejoiced (if that is the word) in the pen name of Charles
Egbert Craddock. She had already become known in the pages
of the *Atlantic Monthly* before she published a first collection of
tales, *In the Tennessee Mountains* (1884). Murfree capitalized

on the brooding peaks, the strong vein of superstition in her people, and the fiercely independent concepts of justice and propriety which contrasted so sharply with those of the lowlander. She also, like her fellows in the field, depended heavily upon dialect, often intentionally comic but sometimes surprisingly eloquent and moving. Murfree's skill at dialog as well as her reliance on melodramatic plot line can be sampled in one of her best stories, "The 'Harnt' that Walks Chilhowee." The dominant character of the story is one Reuben Crabb, "a stunted, one-armed little critter a-ondertakin' ter fight folks and shoot pistols." In one scene the site of his house is remembered, but, as an acquaintance remarks in summarizing Reuben's life and death, it

"ain't thar now, 'kase Sam Grim's brothers burned it ter the ground fur his a-killin' of Sam. That warn't all that war done ter Reuben fur killin' of Sam. The sheriff run Reuben Crabb down this hyar road 'bout a mile from hyar,—mebbe less,—an' shot him dead in the road, jes' whar it forks. Waal, Reuben war in company with another evildoer,—*he* war from the Cross-Roads, an' I furgits what he hed done, but he war a-tryin' ter hide in the mountings, too; an' the sheriff lef' Reuben a-lying thar in the road, while he tries ter ketch up with the t'other; but his horse got a stone in his hoof, an' he los' time, an' hed ter gin it up. An' when he got back ter the forks o' the road whar he had lef' Reuben a-lyin' dead, thar war nuthin' thar 'ceptin' a pool of blood. Waal, he went right on ter Reuben's house, an' them Grim boys hed burnt it ter the ground; but he seen Reuben's brother Joel. An' Joel, he tole the sheriff that late that evenin' he hed tuk Reuben's body out'n the road an' buried it, 'kase it hed been lyin' thar in the road ever sence early in the mornin', an' he couldn't leave it thar all night, an' he hedn't no shelter fur it, since the Grim boys hed burnt down the house. So he war obleeged ter bury it."

This is a ruse; Reuben has survived and, hiding out from the law, becomes the "harnt" that walks the mountain. At the story's close an old acquaintance persuades Reuben to stand trial, gets him acquitted, and takes him to live in his own house, where Reuben proves to be a troublesome and thankless guest. The host is himself an uncouth and ignorant man, but he has performed an act of selfless charity. This "moral gallantry" allows Murfree a final sentimentalizing note of the kind that gratified readers of these "low" tales: "The grace of culture is, in its way, a fine thing, but the best that art can do—the polish of a gentleman—is hardly equal to the best that Nature can do in her higher moods."

The dialect story was also the forte of Joel Chandler Harris, who erased the image of the black as the pious and suffering Uncle Tom by creating the sly and engaging Uncle Remus. Harris's region was the Middle Georgia of the old Cotton Belt, and while he dealt with other types, particularly poor-whites, it was his portraits of plantation blacks that brought him international renown. As a writer for Grady's Atlanta *Constitution,* Harris tried to promote reconciliation and supported the tenets of the New South. But his own roots were strictly rural. The illegitimate son of a woman named Mary Harris and an Irish laborer with whom she lived until he deserted her, young Joel had no hopes for bettering himself until a nearby planter, who was also a lawyer and newspaperman, took on the boy as an apprentice. In his early years Harris witnessed slavery and its abolition; he even got a glimpse of the war as Sherman's army passed by on its march to the sea. He could also directly testify to the plight of both black and white in the harsh years of Reconstruction. His association with ex-slaves opened up for him a body of oral lore which had been largely untouched by earlier southern writers. Though generations of southern children had heard "mammy's" tales and though both southern and northern auditors were often moved by black spirituals and work songs, such material was considered too subliterary to warrant recording. Besides, it was argued, weren't they simply garbled versions of what slaves had heard from whites? The notion that a black could draw from a cultural tradition of his own people was self-evidently false; he had to be *taught* everything, and most masters had found him a slow learner indeed.

Harris himself long was diffident about the literary merits of the poems and tales which he had printed in the *Constitution* and which he first collected in *Uncle Remus: His Songs and His Sayings* (1880). In a letter to Mark Twain, he low-rated himself: "I am perfectly well aware that my book has no basis of literary art to stand upon; I know it is the matter and not the manner that has attracted public attention and won the consideration of people of taste at the North." What attracted attention, of course, was both matter and manner. The matter was pastoral: a way of life that was not grand and snooty but warm, loving, familial. The manner was more artful than it appeared: the accurately rendered accents of an unlettered black man presented without condescension. Harris's skillful use of speech tune and folk metaphor is a far cry from the "Sambo" strain of most earlier black talk in fiction. Something of his appeal still comes across in this passage from the end of "How Mr. Rabbit Was Too Sharp for Mr. Fox." The scene is familiar. Brer Fox, having gotten Brer Rabbit impossibly tangled up with the Tar-Baby, listens to his victim's pleas not to fling him into the brier-patch. Uncle Remus explains:

"Co'se Brer Fox wanter hurt Brer Rabbit bad ez he kin, so he cotch 'im by de behime legs en slung 'im right in de middle er de brier-patch. Dar wuz a considerbul flutter whar Brer Rabbit struck de bushes, en Brer Fox sorter hang 'roun fer ter see w'at wuz gwineter happen. Bimeby he hear somebody call 'im, en way up de hill he see Brer Rabbit settin' cross-legged on a chinkapin log koamin' de pitch outen his har wid a chip. Den Brer Fox know dat he bin swop off mighty bad. Brer Rabbit wuz bleedzed fer ter fling back some er his sass, en he holler out:
      "'Bred en bawn in a brier-patch, Brer Fox—bred en bawn in a brier-patch!' en wid dat he skip out des ez lively ez a cricket in de embers."

How far Harris was aware of his materials as concealed black protest has been a matter for lively debate in recent years. In answering the question as to why the rabbit and not the fox is the trickster-hero, Harris gave an insightful response in the preface to his first collection: "It needs no scientific investigation to show why he [the Negro] selects as his hero the weakest and most harmless of all animals, and brings him out victorious in contests with the bear, the wolf, and the fox." And he did recognize black sources: "It would be presumptious in me to offer an opinion as to the origin of these curious myth-stories; but, if ethnologists should discover that they did not originate with the African, that effect should be accompanied with a good deal of persuasive eloquence." But a nagging question remains: did Uncle Remus outwit his own creator? Is the violent, treacherous, amoral, competitive animal world of the tales a direct analog of black-white relationships? Was Harris psychologically unable to face the deep racial implications of the stories which he so successfully retold?

Such questions cannot be answered with certainty. But, because they have been raised, Harris himself has emerged more clearly in the twentieth century as a man deeply torn by the conflicts of the Reconstruction era, by the desire for "progress" and the attractions of a more Edenic South.

At the height of the local color movement, every southern state could boast of having added strokes to the general panorama. Richard Malcolm Johnson followed Longstreet's lead in finding the Georgia cracker a source for rustic humor. Irwin Russell, who specialized in Negro dialect poetry, produced a great favorite with "Christmas Night in the Quarters" (1878). Even northern writers felt the pull of the Southland. As early as 1873 Mrs. Stowe wrote of her Florida homestead in *Palmetto Leaves;* and Cooper's grandniece, Constance Fenimore Woolson, remembered her days in the Carolinas and Florida in *Rodman the Keeper: Southern Sketches* (1880). But only natives really excelled. Two widely separated locales, Old Virginia and Creole Louisiana, finally produced the two most significant writers to come out of the rejuvenation of southern letters. They were Thomas Nelson Page and George Washington Cable—and they could not have been more different.

Cable's Louisiana is dense, violent, and dominated by its racist attitudes; Page's Virginia is a land of faded glamour and lost dreams, but redeemed and elevated by its harmonious black-white relationships. Of all the defenders of the Lost Cause, Page was the one most beloved by his contemporaries and most scorned by the liberal southern writers who reacted against him in the twentieth century. Born in 1853, Page himself saw little of the Old South in which Nelsons and Pages had flourished; in the years of Reconstruction he sought to restore family prestige and power not by returning to the plantation but by practicing law. Yet the tale of Virginia's legendary past—a Golden Age brought to an end in chivalrous but futile combat—continued to haunt him. His sentimental and highly idealized stories depicting the defeat of southern principles successfully colored and softened attitudes in all sections of the restored Union. Page produced many stories, novels, and other works before his death in 1922; but his classic book, one indispensable in examining the national literary mood, is the collection of six tales, *In Ole Virginia*, published in 1887. Page's forte, like Harris's, was the tale told in Negro dialect. However embarrassing (and sometimes difficult to comprehend) such a rendering of dialog may seem to the reader of today, it was vital in giving the ring of "reality" to his favorite characters, the faithful black servants who knew—and would not give up—their places. The wide success of the book suggests how easily his readers could accept the doctrine of paternalism—though, in fact, ex-slaveholders had been shocked by the "uppity" attitudes of their former property.

The opening story of *In Ole Virginia*, one of the most popular he ever composed, is an epitome of Page's world—and his appeal. The central narrative of "Marse Chan" is framed by a well worn device: a lone traveler on horseback meets a stranger, asks a few perfunctory questions, and is rewarded with a long and stirring narrative. The setting here is the eastern Virginia of many earlier tales; but the time is 1872 and the once splendid mansions which line the narrator's route are falling into decay. His ruminations on mutability are broken into by a mild domestic incident: a Negro is calling home a "noble-looking old orange and white setter," but one now "gray with age, and corpulent with excessive feeding." The dog is "Marse Chan's," and when the narrator inquires about the owner he is given a tale with plot incidents enough to fill a novel.

The story is an unabashed tear-jerker which gains its effect—if it succeeds at all—by the reader's willingness to accept the fundamental goodness of the world which Sam, the black man, recalls so elegiacally. Marse Chan was the heir of a great plantation owner; Sam had been assigned to him as body servant and they had grown up, like brothers, in close association. There appears to be no irony in Sam's words, and certainly none in Page's, as he describes the joys of the old order: " 'Dem wuz good ole times, marster—de bes' Sam ever see! Dey wuz, in fac'! Niggers didn' hed nothing 't all to do—jes' hed to 'ten' to de feedin' an' cleanin' de hosses, an' doin' what de marster tell 'em to do; an' when dey wuz sick, dey had things sont 'em out de house, an' de same doctor come to see 'em whar 'ten' to de white folks when dey wuz po'ly. Dyar warn' no trouble nor nothin'.' "

Now enters the love interest. Chan is smitten at an early age

with the charms of Miss Anne, daughter of a neighboring plantation owner, "Cun'l Chahmb'lin." But the story takes on a Romeo
and Juliet turn, as the fathers of the pair split over politics. Chan,
after being publicly insulted by the colonel, is even forced into a
duel with him; with true nobility he refuses, after the colonel's shot
has missed him, to return the fire, saying only (in Sam's words):
" 'I mek you a present to yo' fam'ly, seh!' " Something of a stickler
in matters of honor, the colonel proclaims himself not satisfied;
and bad blood continues between the two families, until even Miss
Anne denies she ever loved Chan. Chan now escapes into the Civil
War, where he rises to a captaincy, but both he and Anne are
physically suffering from their thwarted romance. Finally the colonel relents. Anne writes Chan that she wants him, and he plans
to marry her on the furlough he will receive after the next big
battle. Naturally, Chan is killed; his homecoming is his burial.
Anne becomes a Confederate nurse, but shortly before Richmond
falls she dies of a fever. The tale ends on a motif out of the
ballad of "Barbara Allen" and a thousand other tales of frustrated
lovers: they are buried side by side in the old churchyard. But
Page adds another, more Victorian, note of weeping religiosity.
Sam asks: " 'An' will yo' please tell me, marster? Dey tells me dat
de Bible sey dyar won' be marryin' nor givin' in marriage in heaven,
but I don' b'lieve it signifies dat—does you?' " The narrator reas-
sures Sam with "the comfort of my earnest belief in some other
interpretation" and gives him a little money, "for which he seemed
humbly grateful." As Sam goes into his cabin, the narrator hears
him call to his wife, " 'Judy, have Marse Chan's dawg got home?' "

Even northern readers like Mrs. Stowe's brother, Henry Ward
Beecher, and Emily Dickinson's "mentor," Thomas Wentworth
Higginson, gladly confessed that they had shed tears over the
tale; and their watery response would seem no more than was appropriate to this calculatedly doleful tale of love cut short. Yet
something else is at work in Page's story. The plot contained nearly
every stereotype of the southern legend: the gallant young man
who falls for his nation; the chilly but eventually faithful lady; the
proud colonel; the duel; the well treated darky; the good times on
the old plantation. Chan and his Miss Anne sprang out of a
vanished time; their deaths symbolized the passing of a never-to-
be-resurrected social order of grace and honor. Surely *these* were

not the people whom the North had sworn to destroy. *They* had not created the slave system; they had only defended their home-land and their way of life. Had the South alone been at fault in the conflict in which such people had given their lives?

For all the derivative quality of his work, for all the choke in the voice when he spoke of the old régime, Page was writing what for him was sacred history. As late as 1887 he gave a famous address on "The Old South" at Washington and Lee University, which he had attended and where the great General of the Confederacy now had his shrine. He undertook, he told his auditors, to prove that "the New South is, in fact, simply the Old South with its energies directed into new lines." Reviewing the history of the slave trade, he charged that the North had hardly been guiltless and that actually it was southerners like Thomas Jefferson who had fought to abolish it. The extinction of slavery seemed assured, Page said, but it "was prevented by the attitude of the Northern Abolitionists. Their furious onslaughts, accompanied by the illegal circulation of literature calculated to excite the negroes to revolt" caused the temper of the South to change. For Page the issue was quite clear: "The real fight was whether the conservative South should, with its doctrine of States' rights, of original State sover-eignty, rule the country according to a literal reading of the Consti-tution, or whether the North should govern according to a more liberal construction, adapted, as it claimed, by necessity to the new and more advanced conditions of the nation." The South had a sacred duty to fight to maintain its institutions, which had produced "a civilization so pure, so noble, that the world to-day holds nothing equal to it." In a few paragraphs, Page summarized the South's case and demanded recognition of its unique achieve-ment:

After less than a generation it has become among friends and enemies the recognized field of romance.

Its chief attribute was conservatism. Others were courage, fidelity, purity, hospitality, magnanimity, honesty, and truth.

Whilst it proudly boasted itself democratic, it was distinctly and avowedly anti-radical—holding fast to those things which were proved, and standing with its conservatism a steadfast bulwark against all novelties and aggressions. . . .

Slavery itself, which proved the spring of woes unnumbered, and which clogged the wheels of progress and withdrew the South from sympathy with the outer world, christianized a race and was the automatic balance-wheel between labor and capital which prevented, on the one hand, the excessive accumulation of wealth, with its attendant perils, and on the other hand prevented the antithesis of the immense pauper class which work for less than the wage of the slave without any of his incidental compensations.

After this traditional attack on northern economy, Page brought himself to endorse reconciliation, but only with the understanding that the Lost Cause be recognized as having been constitutionally sanctioned:

No section of this country more absolutely, loyally, and heartily accepts the fact that slavery and secession can never again become practical questions in this land, than does that which a generation ago flung all its weight into the opposite scale. But to pretend that we did not have the legal, constitutional right to secede from the Union is to stultify ourselves in falsification of history.

If any portion of this nation doubt the South's devotion to the Union, let it attempt to impair the Union. If the South is ever to be once more the leader of this nation, she must cherish the traditional glory of her former station, and prove to the world that her revolution was not a rebellion, but was fought for the principle upon which she was established as her foundation-stone—the sacred right of self-government.

It is no wonder that, with the command of such rhetoric, Page was widely hailed as the keeper of the flame. On the other hand, it would be the lot of Page's contemporary, George Washington Cable, eventually to be branded a "Southern Yankee." There was nothing in Cable's upbringing to suggest such apostasy. Born in 1844 in New Orleans, son of a businessman, Cable had no connection with the plantation culture that Page had made sacred. But he and his family dutifully became Confederates, and young Cable served in the southern army from 1862 to the end of the war. By the postwar years, however, he had begun to doubt that the South had had any legal right to secede, and with this break from the conservative creed he began a steady march toward a liberal view of the slavery issue. Yet little of his crusading zeal is evident in his first book, *Old Creole Days* (1879), a collection of local color stories which had appeared in *Scribner's*. Cable had observed in his native city a kind of exoticism and high melodrama which he rightly guessed would be broadly appealing. Creole culture, with its roots in the Indian, French, and Spanish occupations of the area, was new to American letters, and he became its chief interpreter. That he implicitly—and rather prudishly—condemned its mores was a factor which rubbed nerves at home; but outside readers reveled in the freshness of acquaintanceship with an aristocratic society that owed nothing to the Old Dominion.

By his second book, *The Grandissimes* (1880), Cable had nerved himself to write of something stronger than the peccadilloes of this class-conscious society; he was ready to confront the morality of slavery and the fate of the blacks in the postwar world. His attack was somewhat oblique; he posed the problem through an intricately plotted romance set at the time of the Louisiana Purchase. The situation was a classic one for a sociopolitical novel: that moment when an alien power is about to disrupt an isolated culture smugly secure in the hierarchical structure which it had created over many decades. The American "invaders" are correctly seen by the Creoles as destroyers of their world. Before they are brought under the reign of the new society they are forced to test unchallenged beliefs: their social codes, their pride in family, their land titles, their contemptuous treatment of those of mixed blood. The temporal displacement of the plot line, which allowed for a more colorful backdrop, was not, however, intended to disguise the immediacy of the racial issue; conditions at the time of the Purchase and in Cable's own day clearly were parallel. The worst of contemporary southern prejudice was but an inheritance from the cream of Creole society.

Criticism of the closed mind is carried on in the novel largely through dialogs between a young outsider, an apothecary named Joseph Frowenfeld, and the scion of one of the proudest of the Creole dynasties, Honoré Grandissime. Frowenfeld, a northern immigrant to New Orleans, is the only member of his family who has survived a fever epidemic; he is, therefore, entirely on his own in taking on a man he suspects is incapable of change. Frowenfeld is given to rather platitudinous homilies on slavery and the caste system, and he is particularly censorious of the free sexual alliances which have doomed offspring to be ranked according to their degree of black blood. Even Honoré has a halfbrother, a "free man of color," who bears the same name. The "f.m.c.," as he is called, loves a quadroon woman who, to complicate matters, loves the white Honoré. This is all melodramatic enough, and even daring for its period, but Cable is not out to titillate his readers. Frowenfeld gets a lesson—and a surprise—when he and the white Honoré come upon the despondent "f.m.c." as he is attempting to drown himself, and they foil the attempt. The white Honoré's comment on the intended act reveals his own growing awareness of the horror at the core of Creole culture:

"Ah! Mr. Frowenfeld," said the Creole, suddenly, "if the *immygrant* [as Frowenfeld is] has cause of complaint [about Creole exclusivity], how much more has *that* man! True it is only love for which he would have just now drowned himself; yet what an accusation, my-de'-seh [my dear sir], is his whole life against that 'caste' which shuts him up within its narrow and almost solitary limits! And yet, Mr. Frowenfeld, this people esteem this very same crime of caste the holiest and most precious of their virtues. My-de'-seh, it never occurs to us that in this matter we are interested, and therefore disqualified, witnesses. We say we are not understood; that the jury (the civilized world) renders the decision without viewing the body; that we are judged from a distance. We forget that we ourselves are too *close* to see distinctly, and so continue, a spectacle to civilization, sitting in a horrible darkness, my-de'-seh!" He frowned.

"The shadow of the Ethiopian," said the grave apothecary.

M. Grandissime's quick gesture implied that Frownfeld had said the very word.

"Ah! my-de'-seh, when I try sometimes to stand outside and look at it, I am *ama-aze* at the length, the blackness of that shadow!"

Frowenfeld is finally given the ultimate revelation of that "blackness" when he hears the full story of Bras-Coupé, a slave whose history obsesses the whole Grandissime clan. The tale, which Cable sets at the very center of the book, is too intricate to allow easy summation; what must be said about it, however, is that it remains the most penetrating and powerful parable of slavery written by a southerner in the postwar period. It tells of a true noble savage, an African prince brought in bondage to the Louisiana fields, where it is fated that he will clash with the white owners who try to strip him of his manhood. Eventually he commits a capital crime, striking his master; after putting a curse on the land, he takes refuge in the swamps. The land rots under the spell of the black man, but inevitably he is captured and undergoes the terrible punishment of being lashed and hamstrung—a symbolic castration. The end of the story suffers somewhat from Cable's penchant for the melodramatic and sentimental, but the racial theme is powerful enough to redeem it. Bras-Coupé's master, dying under the curse which the slave has cast, asks to be forgiven. The plea is seconded by the master's wife, who comes to the maimed Bras-Coupé and places her baby within "the hollows of the African's arm." It puts "its hand upon the runaway's face, and the first tears of Bras-Coupé's life, the dying testimony of his humanity, gushed from his eyes. . . . He laid his [hand] tenderly upon the babe's forehead, then removing it, waved it abroad, inaudibly moved his lips, dropped his arm, and closed his eyes. The curse was lifted." Bras-Coupé's death occurs soon after; asked if he knows where he is going, he whispers, " 'To—Africa—' and was gone."

The retelling of this violent tale has become an annual ritual among the Grandissime clan; what Cable implies is that they—by a verbal reenactment of the slave's life, death, and act of forgiveness—are attempting to expiate the guilt of the past which still hangs over their own lives. But they miss the ironic central point: the black man must set the whites free.

In a later essay, Cable remarked, "I meant to make *The Grandissimes* as truly a political work as it ever has been called. . . . I wrote as near to truth and justice as I knew how, upon questions I saw must be settled by calm debate and cannot be settled by force or silence." Cable felt that journalists and politicians did not accurately present the more moderate racial views of his people, and he tried to address a "silent South" which might be encouraged to speak and act more openly. But his reasonable plea for "civil equality" for blacks was too advanced for the mood of the time. It appeared to parrot the old northern line, and it was generally understood that the North would now stay out of the South's handling of its own peculiar social problem. Cable continued to express his liberal ideas both in fiction and in tracts like *The Negro Question,* but his work was to decline in power. In 1885, largely disowned by his own region, he settled in Northampton, Massachusetts. Like Page, he had acknowledged the curse of slavery, but he had argued that the South could now cast off the burden of racism. Like Page, he had urged reconciliation between former enemies. But, unlike Page, he had taken the injunction quite literally: he had turned himself into a northerner.

In late 1884 Cable joined forces with Mark Twain on a four-month lecture tour. The jaunt was a great success—Cable regaled audiences with Creole songs and Twain read from his new book *Huckleberry Finn*—but Cable's primness and piety galled the free-thinking Twain. He had found, he wrote to Howells, that "Cable's gifts of mind are greater & higher than I had suspected"; but he added: "You will never know, never divine, guess, imagine, how loathsome a thing the Christian religion can be made until you come to know & study Cable daily & hourly. . . . in him & his person I have learned to hate all religions. He has taught me to abhor & detest the Sabbath-day & hunt up new & troublesome ways to dishonor it."

By the time of this tour Mark Twain had lived away from the South since 1861, and he had moved toward contempt for the South's "religion": its code of chivalry which masked horrors like feuds and lynchings under the proud badge of "honor." Of course, like all his views, Twain's attitudes toward the region were marked by riotous contradictions, by conflicting emotions which drove him to picture the South both as the pastoral Eden of his boyhood and as a present-day cultural and moral wasteland. In the 1880s and '90s the latter view was predominant. This Twain thundered and blasted away as a self-proclaimed anti-"Southron," but it is obvious that he could not have been so caustically brilliant if he had not himself once embraced the South's dogmas about race and caste. His father was a Virginian with the airs of the gentry, his mother a Kentuckian; the family had moved on to the slave state of Missouri, where Samuel Langhorne Clemens was born in 1835. The young man emigrated to the West, where he made his reputation; in later years he built homes in the East, where he made his fortune. But three of his best books—*Life on the Mississippi, Adventures of Huckleberry Finn,* and *Pudd'nhead Wilson*—are set in the Southland he had known; and one fat volume of previously unpublished writings is devoted to "the

Matter of Hannibal," the small river town of his youth. He had missed the Civil War because, after a brief stint as a Confederate militiaman, he had decamped to join his Unionist brother in Nevada. His imaginative return to the place of his youth was not to come until 1875, when he contributed to the *Atlantic Monthly* a series of sketches called "Old Times on the Mississippi," which glorified the cub pilot days when he first learned to "read the book" of the great river. There is little direct confrontation of the slave-holding South here; and in his "boys' book" of the next year, *The Adventures of Tom Sawyer,* nostalgic recollections of his river town are disturbed by terrors which are more melodramatic than sociological.

Twain's continuation of his memoirs, however, is another matter. *Life on the Mississippi* (1883), written after he had toured the South for the first time since 1861, contains untrammeled assaults on the flossier versions of southern chivalric legend which had been flooding postwar periodicals. In his view, the South had been the victim not only of chattel slavery but of a slavishness of mind which Twain largely attributed to the enthralling prose of Sir Walter Scott. In a characteristic reading of history, he argued that, though the French Revolution and Napoleonic wars had involved real crimes, the world was in their debt for "great and permanent services to liberty, humanity, and progress." In a familiar passage which prefigures the style and technique of H. L. Mencken, Twain then ripped into the Old South's cherished romancer:

Then comes Sir Walter Scott with his enchantments, and by his single might checks this wave of progress, and even turns it back; sets the world in love with dreams and phantoms; with decayed and swinish forms of religion; with decayed and degraded systems of government; with the sillinesses and emptinesses, sham grandeurs, sham gauds, and sham chivalries of a brainless and worthless long-vanished society. He did measureless harm; more real and lasting harm, perhaps, than any other individual that ever wrote. Most of the world has now outlived good part of these harms, though by no means all of them; but in our South they flourish pretty forcefully still. Not so forcefully as half a generation ago, perhaps, but still forcefully. There, the genuine and wholesome civilization of the nineteenth century is curiously confused and commingled with the Walter Scott Middle-Age sham civilization, and so you have practical common-sense, progressive ideas, and progressive works, mixed up with the duel, the inflated speech, and the jejune romanticism of an absurd past that is dead, and out of charity ought to be buried. But for the Sir Walter disease, the character of the Southerner—or Southron, according to Sir Walter's starchier way of phrasing it—would be wholly modern, in place of modern and mediæval mixed, and the South would be fully a generation further advanced than it is. It was Sir Walter that made every gentleman in the South a major or a colonel, or a general, or a judge, before the war; and it was he, also, that made these gentlemen value these bogus decorations. For it was he that created rank and caste down there, and also reverence for rank and caste, and pride and pleasure in them. Enough is laid on slavery, without fathering upon it these creations and contributions of Sir Walter.

It is admittedly a "wild proposition," Twain went on, but "Sir Walter had so large a hand in making Southern character, as it existed before the war, that he is in great measure responsible for the war."

Twain's diatribe is without real substance as historical analysis; but it is eloquent proof of an author's belief that his works create, rather than reflect, the mood of a period. Scott had been, after all, but one element in the medieval revival which had swept over much of Europe and America. What his romances did, fundamentally, was to confirm for many Southerners the essential rightness of a caste system and a chivalric ideal; that confirmation came, however, from other sources as well.

In his eagerness to diagnose the "Sir Walter disease," Twain was not very perceptive or accurate about past and present southern writing. He scorned the "wordy, windy, flowery 'eloquence'" of much antebellum American writing, and he had to confess that it "was the fashion in both sections of the country." But he had to twist literary history to bring his final charge against the pernicious effect of romanticism upon the South. In prewar days, he asserted, "the South was able to show as many well-known literary names, proportioned to population, as the North could." "But," he went on, "a change has come, and there is no opportunity now for a fair competition between North and South. For the North has thrown out that old inflated style, whereas the Southern writer still clings to it—clings to it and has a restricted market for his wares, as a consequence. There is as much literary talent in the South, now, as ever there was, of course; but its work can gain but slight currency under present conditions; the authors write for the past, not the present; they use obsolete forms and a dead language." Was Twain really so blind about the enormous vogue for a southern literature about the southern past? Probably he had simply come to hate the widespread acceptance of the *content* of southern writing; critique of style was a poor argument, for even in the North "realism" was hardly the dominant mode in most popular fiction. Twain reserved praise only for Cable and Harris—"two of the very few Southern authors who do not write in the Southern style." Yet, illogically, it was their command of local dialects that he praised unreservedly. What he did not mention was the attraction for him of their relatively radical beliefs on the racial issue.

In his next major work, *Huckleberry Finn* (1885), Twain managed to make his points less frenetically by adopting a new distancing device, allowing an unsophisticated boy to speak his thoughts in a rough vernacular tongue. Though the novel rises above the southern scene to pose the large philosophical issue of man's freedom to choose his own course, its satirical attack is often quite specific and local. The world of Huck Finn's vision is a moral desert, where slavery and bigotry are the bedrock of "sivilization." Huck's own movement toward humaneness—toward his recognition that Jim, though black and a slave, is a man—is slow in pace; and, in the crucial scene where he decides not to report Jim as a runaway, he still acknowledges the weight of his culture's central beliefs. Conscience, the instilled voice of society, tells Huck that to aid Jim is a damnable act; and he makes his decision in defiance: "'All right, then, I'll *go* to hell.'" As Twain sets up the mood of the scene, we are clearly meant to applaud Huck's act; but all the events of the river journey make it certain that Huck already *is* in hell, that once off the river he and Jim are forever outcasts from Christian society. Twain knew this landscape from his own early and recent experiences, but his choice of targets also shows the pressure upon him of several decades of the South's endeavor to create a favorable self-image. Romantic tastes are mocked in the name of the wrecked steamboat aboard which Huck and Jim have their first adventure—the "Walter Scott." The intellectual aridity and cultural shallowness of the gentry are pilloried in the chapter devoted to Huck's description of the "tastefulness" of the Grangerford home. But Twain's greatest scorn is expended on the Old South's pride in its stratified society, and he makes Huck the mouthpiece for some ironically edged words: "Col. Grangerford was a gentleman, you see. He was a gentleman all over; and so was his family. He was well born, as the saying is, and that's worth as much in a man as it is in a horse, so the Widow Douglas said, and nobody ever denied that she was of the first aristocracy in our town." Their code of honor has involved the Grangerfords in a bloody feud with the Shepherdsons—"another clan of aristocracy" which is as "high-toned and well born and rich and grand." Huck tries to learn from young Buck, one of the Grangerford lads, what initiated the quarrel; and he gets a lesson in the niceties of aristocratic behavior when Buck tells him: "'It started thirty year ago, or som'ers along there. There was trouble 'bout something, and then a lawsuit to settle it; and the suit went agin one of the men, and so he up and shot the man that won the suit—which he would naturally do, of course. Anybody would.'" Huck flees the scene as the two families are wiping each other out in a culminating gunfight; but his raft drifts him into another locale in which Twain makes his most ferocious assault upon caste —the Boggs-Sherburn episode.

Boggs, a harmless old drunk, has publicly mocked Colonel Sherburn, and the colonel, after warning Boggs of retaliation if he doesn't shut up, has shot him dead on the street. A lynching party is gotten up and confronts Sherburn at his home. Sherburn's defiance of the mob, and his denunciation of the southern code of justice, is all the more cutting because it comes from the mouth of one who had been raised in the system:

"The idea of *you* lynching anybody! It's amusing. The idea of you thinking you had pluck enough to lynch a *man*! . . . Why a *man's* safe in the hands of ten thousand of your kind—as long as it's daytime and you're not behind him.

"Do I know you? I know you clear through. I was born and raised in the South, and I've lived in the North; so I know the average all around. The average man's a coward. . . . Your newspapers call you a brave people so much that you think you *are* braver than any other people—whereas you're just *as* brave, and no braver. Why don't your juries hang murderers? Because they're afraid the man's friends will shoot them in the back, in the dark—and it's just what they *would* do.

"So they always acquit; and then a *man* goes in the night, with a hundred masked cowards at his back and lynches the rascal. Your mistake is, that you didn't bring a man with you; that's one mistake, and the other is that you didn't come in the dark and fetch your masks. . . . Now the thing for *you* to do is to droop your tails and go home and crawl in a hole. If any real lynching's going to be done it will be done in the dark, Southern fashion; and when they come they'll bring their masks and fetch a *man* along. Now *leave—*."

The high rhetoric and the sneering analysis of mob psychology are more than a Huck could have managed; and Twain returns us to Huck's voice in his toneless comment: "I could a stayed if I wanted to, but I didn't want to."

The final chapters of *Huckleberry Finn*—the elaborate plot to "free" Jim from his mock captivity at Phelps Farm—have seemed to many readers only a tediously extended parody of the Scott-Dumas school which degrades the character of Jim himself. But they properly take us back to the world of Tom Sawyer, that "good bad boy" who can face life only by turning its horrifying realities into containable illusions. At the end of the book Huck stands defeated: he knows that the Tom Sawyers of this world will prevail and that their ethic will never allow blacks and whites to live together in a bond of brotherhood. Twain allows him only a futile gesture of escape; he will, Huck tells us, "light out for the Territory ahead of the rest, because Aunt Sally she's going to adopt me and sivilize me, and I can't stand it. I been there before." So had Twain. And, by this time, so have we.

Twain's last major use of southern material was in *Pudd'nhead Wilson* (1894), a near-botch of a book which is saved largely by his unusually frank portrayal of a mulatto woman character, Roxana. Twain tells us that he had started to write a farce about Siamese twins; the farce had begun to turn into a tragedy when he introduced Roxana and had her switch her illegitimate baby with the newborn son of her master. The "tragedy" is said to be that of Pudd'nhead Wilson, the freethinker and longtime outcast citizen of the village who, by the end of the book, has made himself a hero by winning a sensational murder case and has become a "success."

But the real tragedy is man's notion that he can escape his heredity and environment, and Twain again employs the South's illusions about its society to illustrate his case. The boys exchanged in the cradle meet suitably ironic fates: the "base-born" Tom, raised as a white, is betrayed by the "nigger" in him, is unmasked, and is literally "sold down the river." The "high-born" Chambers, raised as a slave, succeeds to a white man's estate; but he cannot free himself from the manners and attitudes of the black he has thought himself to be.

For once Twain had the temerity to expose the most embarrassing, and the most hushed-up, aspect of slavery: the sexual exploitation of the black woman by white masters. Roxana herself is the offspring of miscegenation: "Only one-sixteenth of her was black, and that sixteenth did not show. . . . To all intents and purposes Roxy was as white as anybody, but the one-sixteenth of her which was black outvoted the other fifteen parts and made her a negro. She was a slave and salable as such." Roxy has had a liaison with one of the white grandees of the village; their child, therefore, was "thirty-one parts white, and he, too, was a slave, and by a fiction of law and custom a negro." Twain's contempt for the Old Dominion's chivalry—the "F.F.V.'s" who dominate the town's society—now had grown to the point where he could treat them with pure mockery, burdening them with fanciful names like "Colonel Cecil Burleigh Essex" and "Percy Northumberland Driscoll." Against such people Roxy tries to act as a moral foil; she works herself out of slavery and tries—by placing her own baby in the white heir's cradle—to tilt the balance of her black/white world. Yet Roxy too remains in thrall to the pervasive racism. In a scene in which she reveals to her son the truth of his parentage, she tells him proudly: "'You ain't got no 'casion to be shame' o' yo' father, *I* kin tell you. He wuz the highest quality in dis whole town—ole Virginny stock. Fust famblies, he wuz.'" And later, when her son refuses to fight a duel, she stings him with the taunt that blood will tell: "'It's de nigger in you, dat's what it is. Thirty-one parts o' you is white, en on'y part nigger, en dat po' little one part is yo' *soul*.'"

Mark Twain was a humane man, and in his private life as Samuel Clemens he was a steadfast advocate of civil rights for black people. But philosophically he increasingly became skepti-

cal that anyone in the whole "damned human race" was capable
of salvation. The notion of individual freedom was the final folly
of a species which could escape neither history nor biology. Twain
may well have seemed what William Dean Howells called him:
"the most desouthernized Southerner I ever knew." But his fictions
betray the real truth: he could not go home again, but that home
forever burned in his blood. It was "the Southerner" in him that
gave him his most powerful themes.

The last years of the nineteenth century saw the fading of the local
color movement; but they were marked by two ironic events in
southern letters. The first was that a black man won fame by writing about black people without revealing his own racial identity.
The other was that a woman won notoriety by frankly revealing
what it meant to be a woman in her time and place.

The black author, Charles W. Chesnutt (1858–1932), had
broken into print in the *Atlantic Monthly* in 1887 with a local
color story set in North Carolina. A number of other tales followed, and in 1899 he issued the two collections upon which his
present reputation rests: *The Conjure Woman* and *The Wife of
His Youth*. That his publishers did not reveal Chesnutt's color was
not, as one might suspect, the result of any fear of prejudicial reaction. Their silence was meant as compliment: his work was just
as good as that of any white author. Chesnutt himself did not wish
to be known as a "Negro writer"; he sought recognition as a
person who had mastered the literary craft of the local colorists
as it had been practiced in prestigious periodicals. Yet he did
manage to present a black point of view without creating the direct
emotional confrontation quite possible in this decade of stricter
"Jim Crow" laws. Chesnutt was not the first southern Negro to
write fiction (a fugitive slave named William Wells Brown had
produced a sensational protest novel as early as 1853) but he was
the first to have his work initially judged on its own merits. He
wrote on into the twentieth century, but his later and more frankly
"black" productions were a disappointment, both to favorable
critics like Howells and to Chesnutt himself, who had hoped to
contribute to the bettering of racial relations.

The continuing conservatism of taste was to be felt by Kate
Chopin (1851–1904), who dared to make the sexual desires of

a woman the main subject of her novel *The Awakening* (1899). Before this book Chopin had published a number of local color stories of the French-American South, which had been collected in *Bayou Folk* (1894) and *A Night in Acadie* (1897). Her work in this vein is best illustrated by the frequently anthologized "Désirée's Baby," a story of unwitting miscegenation in which the mother is cast out by her husband and drowns both herself and her child. But the story is given an unexpected twist: not the mother but the father turns out to have been the carrier of Negro blood. In 1890 Chopin experimented with longer fiction in *At Fault*, but this rather weak production would be forgotten in the attention given *The Awakening*. This second novel, which details the life and death of a woman who, tiring of her husband, seeks sexual satisfaction outside marriage, proved too "European" for contemporary critics; after one reprinting it disappeared, only to be rediscovered and properly reevaluated in recent years. Its frankness and its cool attitude toward extramarital gratification make it unique for its period. Chopin had been born in Missouri during the days of the Old South; she lived through the whole of the New South and dutifully did her part for her region in her short stories. But in her last novel she had the courage to look toward a newer South, one in which women writers could at last free their characters from that stultifying stereotype, the Southern Lady.

The Legacy

WHAT HAD "the South" meant? What were the portents for its future? As the nineteenth century ebbed away, the problem of maintaining a regional identity engaged a number of commentators who were now taking retrospective sweeps across the preceding decades. The question of continued support of "Southern literature" in particular taxed the pens of those who had recently founded what have proved to be two of the most distinguished and long-lasting of southern periodicals, the *Sewanee Review* and the *South Atlantic Quarterly.* The latter editorially took a fairly pragmatic line, repeating arguments that Poe and Simms would have found familiar: southerners were not a book-reading nor, gallingly, a book-buying class. How could they be made to contribute more than goodwill? A more ambitious study was contributed to the first issue by Henry N. Snyder, who called for no less than "The Reconstruction of Southern Literary Thought." Snyder is clear-eyed in elucidating the failures of the Old South. Pointing out that "we always hear of *Southern* literature and *Southern* writers as if we had no share in the larger name, American," he goes right to the roots:

This localizing designation of literary effort in the South—at once a distinction and a reproach—came out of those well known social, political, and economic conditions which, before the war, kept the South sensitive to repel outside influences and arrogant—this word is not too strong—to maintain the high value of whatever it regarded as sectionally its own. This spirit was applied to literature as it was applied to everything else, and the result was the multiplying of books and periodicals under the emphatic and rather challenging title of "Southern." But the significant thing about this cry of the South for a literature which should be particularly its own—its own as distinguished from that produced elsewhere in the nation—is that the cry was the sign of the excessive intellectual loneliness and detachment forced upon the South by the very conditions of its life.

Snyder rejoices that life opened up in the postwar years; it is, he adds with some pride, "a matter of general recognition to say now that Southern writers and Southern themes have, for the last ten years or more, monopolized the pages of the leading magazines. The avidity on the part of the outside world for everything Southern has had the important use of creating an active demand, which the Southern writer feels he must supply, and that he alone can supply in a just and adequate way." Snyder makes a quick survey of the artistic quality of this movement, only to reveal that his own taste is resolutely genteel and formed upon literary myths. One judgment will suffice: "The negro in his relationship to his white masters, the romance and nobility of that splendid Virginia civilization of which both were a part, the beating of the fiery fury of the war upon this civilization, the pain of building anew upon its ruins, are made vitally real things in the novels of Mrs. Burton Harrison and of Thomas Nelson Page." But Snyder is more forward-looking in his recognition that southern universities are beginning to develop a scientific approach to history; and he hopes that the work of such scholars "stands for the coming of a larger intellectual atmosphere in which one may think with absolute independence."

Like most commentators at the turn of the century, Snyder is a mixture of progressivism in the social sphere and conservatism in the literary. Though the championship by William Dean Howells of certain southern authors is sometimes mentioned with self-satisfaction, his campaign for realism in letters is generally ignored. The primary aim of art is still seen in idealistic terms; it must be inspirational and express lofty goals, must draw upon the best of the regional past to reassure southern readers that they have not lost their peculiar identity.

Something of this same sort of tug between fealty to the New South and attraction to the virtues of an old régime can be observed in an essay by C. Alphonso Smith, who was to become a pioneer in the academic study of southern writing at the University of North Carolina. Smith's article appeared in an 1898 issue of the *Sewanee Review*; it is titled (as how many before it?) "The Possibilities of the South in Literature." The argument may sound a bit muddled to us, for it begins in a tone of New South polemic and ends as Old South hagiography. But it is a revealing insight into the mind of a southerner placed between two worlds, one indeed half-dead, the other already powerful in its adolescence. Smith sounds resolutely progressivist as he begins:

Those persons who proclaim that literature has but meagre opportunities in the South because the South is too much absorbed in her new industrial life are usually those who do not know what literature is or what the literary life implies. Such persons look upon literature as a mere diversion, savoring more of artifice than of art, more of sentimentality than of sentiment. . . .

It is true that the South has entered upon her period of industrialism, this period dating from about the year 1870. Statistics show that at that time the South began a career of unparalleled material prosperity. She began to lead a new life, not so picturesque or princely as the old ante-bellum life, but as Mr. [Henry W.] Grady says, a more strenuous life, a broader and a better life.

Now it is a significant fact that the new movement in Southern literature dates also from 1870. The coincidence is not accidental; it is a confirmation of the truth that literature is the expression of life, and that there is no antagonism, therefore, between industrial activity and literary activity.

And he goes on to forecast that "an impartial study of the present industrial and economic conditions of the South, with the rich promise that they enfold, leads to the conclusion that greater literary triumphs are in store." With rather pleasant hyperbole, Smith suggests that the South is now historically in the same state England was in just before the Elizabethan period began; and that age "was great in letters because it was great in life."

The sun of true literary greatness is only now about to dawn, and Smith chides mourners of the old culture: "In oratory and statesmanship the Old South challenges comparison with any section of our country, but her purely literary output did not attain national, far less international, recognition; it was, as a whole, provincial." The cause for this failure of belles lettres Smith links to the refusal of the South in the 1830s to join England and the North in the industrial revolution, since the new spirit of that age awakened first-rate literary talent abroad and in New England. Why, he asks, "did not the South respond to this great literary and industrial movement? Because her intellectual energies were being more and more absorbed in defense of her constitutional views and her cherished institutions. . . . Her industrial system, based on slave labor, stood as a barrier to the new industrial movement; and the enforced defense of this system . . . threw literature into the background and brought oratory and statesmanship to the front."

The Civil War proved that in the South's hand "the sword was mightier than the pen." The defeated region could thank "the God of battles that slavery is no more." And yet it is true that the "New South inherits the virtues of the Old, for she is the child of the Old. She will listen to no praise, she will accept no honors, that must be bought by repudiation of her past. As she looks toward the future with courage in her heart and confidence on her brow, she yet cherishes above price the record of courage and endurance that the Old South has bequeathed to her." Thomas Nelson Page could hardly have put it better.

With the pieties observed, Smith now hauls himself back to his main theme: the linking of material progress and high-quality literary productivity: "With new economic ideas, with an ever-increasing development of her natural resources, with a more flexible attitude toward manual labor, and more enlightened methods of public education, there has come a literary inspiration impossible before." He calls the roll of the recent worthies: Lanier, Irwin Russell, Maurice Thompson, Harris, Mary N. Murfree, Cable, Page, James Lane Allen. Up to this point in his essay, the reader might well assume that Smith was envisioning a future southern literature of strong social-political content. But not at all. His estimate of the achievement of the postwar galaxy is straight out of the genteel, romantic tradition; the new literature, Smith proudly asserts, has "thrown open a new field; it has revealed an unsuspected wealth of beauty and suggestiveness; it is the reflection of a life responsive to romance and rich in undeveloped possibilities." What possibilities? Why, for one, the contact of French and Spanish civilizations, which "has left a rich deposit of romantic

episode that Southern writers are only beginning to appreciate."
And, even better: "There is one other advantage possessed by
Southern writers which cannot be overlooked in even the most
cursory attempt to forecast the future of American literature. It
is a truism to say that the war meant far more to the South than
to the North. To the North it meant the preservation of the Union
and the abolition of slavery. To the South it meant decimated families, smoking homesteads, and the passing forever of a civilization
unique in human history. *But literature loves a lost cause, provided
honor be not lost.*"

In his final paragraph, Smith looked into his crystal ball for
the future and found—the past: "I do not doubt that the strange
century that is almost upon us will bring to the South new themes
and inspirations, but for the present Southern literature will continue to be retrospective. Our Walter Scott will have to come before our Charles Dickens." It is worth noting that these words
were written within one year after the publication of the first novel
of Ellen Glasgow, who—to the contrary—would proclaim that
"what the South most needs is blood and irony," and who, in a
long career, would attempt to give it both.

But certainly the "strange century" that loomed ahead fulfilled
several of Smith's anticipations of the "retrospective" strain. Walter Scott did live again. From Mary Johnston's *The Long Roll* to
Margaret Mitchell's *Gone With the Wind,* the Old South and its
Lost Cause were glamorized, sanitized, and merchandised. The
"South" became as salable a commodity as the "Old West"; its
symbols would suffer debasement into gimcrack souvenirs. All
across the land the benign face of the southern colonel atop his
fried chicken outlet gazed down at cars flaunting that banner under which many once had died—the battle flag of the Confederacy.
And what region was more ripe for the ultimate vulgarization of
the Hollywood film? One of the dream factory's earliest epics—
and one of its biggest money-makers—was "The Birth of a Nation," a spectacle as inaccurate in its history as it was authentic in
its blatant racism.

The history of the South is of course no different from that of
any other region in its vulnerability to being twisted for ideological
or commercial purposes. If all that the nineteenth-century South
had managed to do was to furnish material for mindless romanc-

ers, white supremacists, and genealogists hot on the scent of a Cavalier forebear, we could properly relegate it to the anatomizers of popular culture. What makes it vital to the literary historian is the fact that out of its matrix there emerged in the 1920s a movement that is comparable in scope and brilliance to the northern flowering of the 1850s. In fiction, poetry, drama, and criticism the South all at once achieved what it could not have dreamed of a century before: a literature that was not only distinctively "southern" but also universal in its implications.

The "Southern Renascence" is not without its mysteries. Why does genius suddenly flourish at any time, in any place? But it is not entirely inexplicable. Most of those writers who came to maturity in the 1920s had been born around the turn of the century, before the South had fully confronted industrialism and modernism of thought. The peculiarities of the region which were embalmed in history, literature, and folkways were part of the baggage which they carried into a new era. They were the offspring of a place and a time, but they had to grow into adults in a world they would never have made. The contrast led them to ponder deeply the nature of their inheritance. A modern historian has tabulated the unique elements of southern history which had given them a special vision: the region had suffered poverty in a land of plenty; had known failure and defeat in a nation that worships success; had been preoccupied with guilt in the face of the legend of American innocence; and, fearing abstraction, had maintained a strong sense of place and of belonging. Simply by being children of this South, these writers were forced by their pasts to come to terms with their modern selves. And at last the meaning of the legacy was realized in works of great power. What the southern experience had bequeathed them was, in the words of the greatest of them, William Faulkner, a profounder awareness of "the problems of the human heart in conflict with itself."

Bibliographical Note

In the past few decades the study of southern literature in all periods has become a major academic undertaking. Though the chief research centers are southern-based, they are far from being southern-biased; scholars are finally able to examine a regional literature dispassionately without undergoing the criticism of regional patriots. The criticism, biography, and history which they have produced is immense; a basic aid to sorting it out is Louis D. Rubin, Jr., *A Bibliographical Guide to the Study of Southern Literature* (Baton Rouge, 1969). A follow-up volume is *Southern Literature, 1968–1975,* edited by Jerry T. Williams (Boston, 1978). An annual bibliography, published in the spring issue of the *Mississippi Quarterly,* brings this information up to date. Useful information about current activities can also be found in the *News-Letter of the Society for the Study of Southern Literature* (currently issued by Mississippi State University).

In writing a concise survey of literature in the South before 1900, I have been very conscious of how much I have had to omit. I have attempted to put together a coherent essay by concentrating upon those whom I take to be key figures, whatever the intrinsic quality of their work. I have emphasized what seems to me most "southern" in the authors I have surveyed; inevitably, this approach has meant neglect of the work which many did in other areas. Fortunately there is a long and authoritative study which will help to fill in these and other gaps: Jay B. Hubbell's *The South in American Literature, 1607–1900* (Durham, N.C., 1954). I am indebted to this work throughout my own essay; a number of brief quotations, otherwise unidentified, are taken from this source. I have also quoted texts from one of the best one-volume anthologies, *Southern Writing, 1585–1920* (New York, 1970), edited, with excellent introductions and headnotes, by

Richard Beale Davis, C. Hugh Holman, and Louis D. Rubin, Jr. A later anthology, *The Literary South* (New York, 1979), is edited by Rubin alone. Two earlier collections remain standard: Edd W. Parks, editor, *Southern Poets* (New York, 1936) and Gregory L. Paine, editor, *Southern Prose Writers* (New York, 1947). A guide to the whole range of southern authors is *Southern Writers: A Biographical Dictionary* (Baton Rouge, 1979), edited by Robert Bain, Joseph M. Flora, and Louis D. Rubin, Jr. A useful discussion both of accomplishment and of remaining problems in the field is *Southern Literary Study: Problems and Possibilities*, edited by Rubin and Holman (Chapel Hill, N.C., 1975). Of the journals which regularly print articles on the South, I especially recommend the *Southern Literary Journal* (Chapel Hill, N.C.); its review section is both dependable and stimulating. In the notes on individual chapters which follow I have identified the sources of my quotations; because of space limitations, I have listed only those articles and books which have most directly contributed to my remarks.

Chapter 1

Texts (except for Byrd's) are from the Davis-Holman-Rubin anthology. I have used the modernized form of Byrd's writings in Louis B. Wright, editor, *The Prose Works of William Byrd of Westover* (Cambridge, Mass., 1966). For general background, I owe most to two works by a foremost scholar, Richard Beale Davis: *Intellectual Life in Jefferson's Virginia, 1790–1830* (Chapel Hill, 1964), and *Literature and Society in Early Virginia, 1608–1840* (Baton Rouge, 1973). Davis has now crowned his work with the three-volume *Intellectual Life in the Colonial South, 1585–1763* (Knoxville, 1978). The appeal of the Lost Colony to literary mythmakers is analyzed by Robert D. Arner in "The Romance of Roanoke: Virginia Dare and the Lost Colony in American Literature," *Southern Literary Journal* (Spring, 1978); the quoted phrase is Arner's. A similar inquiry into the Smith-Pocahontas story is Philip Young's "The Mother of Us All: Pocahontas Reconsidered," *Kenyon Review* (Summer, 1962). The standard work on Smith is Philip L. Barbour, *The Three Worlds of Captain John Smith* (Boston, 1964). My comments on Byrd draw from Wright's introduction to the *Prose Works* and from two studies by R. B. Davis, one in *Literature and Society*, the other in Everett Emerson, editor, *Major Writers of Early American Literature* (Madison, Wis., 1972).

On the idea of the southern "garden," see Lewis P. Simpson, *The Dispossessed Garden* (Athens, Ga., 1975).

Chapter 2

The most thorough coverage of the South is the ten-volume *A History of the South* (Baton Rouge, 1947–1967), edited by Wendell H. Stephenson and E. Merton Coulter. Of the several excellent one-volume histories of the South, I have most often referred to Clement Eaton, *The Growth of Southern Civilization* (New York, 1961) and Francis B. Simkins and Charles P. Roland, *A History of the South* (New York, 1972). Other works I have found useful are: Clement Eaton, *The Mind of the Old South* (Baton Rouge, 1967); William R. Taylor, *Cavalier and Yankee* (Garden City, 1963); Rollin G. Osterweis, *Romanticism and Nationalism in the Old South* (New Haven, 1949), which is a bit heavy on the Scott influence. Revisionist histories of slavery have been numerous in recent years; of those which I have read I have found most provocative two works by Eugene D. Genovese: *The World the Slaveholders Made* (New York, 1969) and *Roll, Jordan, Roll: The World the Slaves Made* (New York, 1974). The *Southern Literary Journal* regularly runs articles covering individual southern periodicals; the article on the *Southern Literary Messenger* by Robert D. Jacobs (Fall, 1969) is an accurate and informative survey. I have also read through the original file. The question of Poe as southerner is treated in most of the standard studies; a brief discussion which touches upon the key points is in Rubin and Holman, *Southern Literary Study*, pp. 102ff.

Chapter 3

Quotations are drawn from William Wirt, *The Letters of the British Spy* (Chapel Hill, 1970), with an introduction by R. B. Davis; George Tucker, *The Valley of Shenandoah* (Chapel Hill, 1970), introduction by Donald R. Noble; John Pendleton Kennedy, *Swallow Barn* (New York, 1962), introduction by William S. Osborne; Nathaniel Beverley Tucker, *The Partisan Leader* (Chapel Hill, 1971), introduction by C. Hugh Holman; William A. Caruthers, *The Knights of the Golden Horse-Shoe* (Chapel Hill, 1970). My commentary draws from the introductions to these volumes, from my own *John Pendleton Kennedy* (New York, 1966), and from Curtis Carroll Davis, *Chronicler of the Cavaliers* (Richmond, 1953).

Chapter 4

I have used material from my *William Gilmore Simms* (New York, 1962); quotations are from my edition of *The Yemassee* (New York, 1964). Of the many recent articles, I have found a particularly good survey and critique in Simone Vauthier, "Of Time and the South: The Fiction of William Gilmore Simms," *Southern Literary Journal* (Fall, 1972). For the Southwestern humorists I have relied on three anthologies: Kenneth S. Lynn, *The Comic Tradition in America* (Garden City, 1958); Hennig Cohen and William B. Dillingham, editors, *Humor of the Old Southwest* (Boston, 1964); and John Q. Anderson, *With the Bark On* (Nashville, 1967).

Chapter 5

I have again made use of my book on Simms in this chapter. Quotations from Simms letters here and elsewhere are from *The Letters of William Gilmore Simms*, edited by Mary C. Simms Oliphant, Alfred T. Odell, and T. C. Duncan Eaves (Columbia, S.C., 1952–1956). Quotations from Simms's works are from the original editions. Articles from which I have drawn information on the *Uncle Tom's Cabin* controversy are Barrie Hayne, "Yankee in the Patriarchy: T. B. Thorpe's Reply to *Uncle Tom's Cabin*," *American Quarterly* (Summer, 1968) and Cushing Strout, "*Uncle Tom's Cabin* and the Portent of Millenium," *Yale Review* (Spring 1968). My quotations from *The Planter's Northern Bride* and some factual material are from the edition introduced by Rhoda Coleman Ellison (Chapel Hill, 1970). I have used the first edition of Helper's *The Impending Crisis* (New York, 1857). Good critical assessments of the Old South in literature are Edd W. Parks, editor, *Southern Poets* and *Ante-Bellum Southern Literary Critics* (Athens, Ga., 1962); Gregory L. Paine, editor, *Southern Prose Writers*. My remarks on the drama are brief because I find that, while theater flourished, native drama was relatively puerile. An excellent bibliographical guide, including play lists, is by Charles S. Watson, in Rubin, editor, *Bibliographical Guide*.

Chapter 6

Books which directly treat the Civil War and literature are: Robert A. Lively, *Fiction Fights the Civil War* (Chapel Hill, 1957); Edmund

Wilson, *Patriotic Gore* (New York, 1962); and Daniel Aaron, *The Unwritten War* (New York, 1973). "The Conquered Banner" is quoted from *Father Ryan's Poems* (Baltimore, 1881). Texts of Timrod and Hayne are from the Davis-Holman-Rubin anthology. My remarks on Lanier owe much to Charles R. Anderson, editor, *Sidney Lanier: Poems and Letters* (Baltimore, 1969).

Chapter 7

Historical works which I have used are C. Vann Woodward, *Origins of the New South* (Baton Rouge, 1951) and *The Strange Career of Jim Crow* (New York, 1966). Two anthologies of local color writing contain the texts which I have quoted: Harry R. Warfel and G. Harrison Orians, editors, *American Local-Color Stories* (New York, 1941) and Claude M. Simpson, editor, *The Local Colorists* (New York, 1960). The Harris story is from *Uncle Remus: His Songs and Sayings* (New York, 1880). Page's address is reprinted in *The Old South* (New York, 1892). Passages from *The Grandissimes* are from the original edition; for Cable's political writings I have used Arlin Turner, editor, *The Negro Question* (New York, 1958). Twain's letter to Howells is in Henry Nash Smith and William M. Gibson, editors, *Mark Twain–Howells Letters* (New York, 1960); the texts of the novels are from the "Author's National Edition" (New York, 1907–1918). The fullest and most convincing study of Twain and his region is Arthur G. Pettit, *Mark Twain and the South* (Lexington, Ky., 1974).

Epilog

The search for the central theme in southern history is discussed in Frank E. Vandiver, editor, *The Idea of the South* (Chicago, 1964). The final paragraph draws from C. Vann Woodward, "The Search for Southern Identity" in *The Burden of Southern History* (Baton Rouge, 1968). Faulkner's remark is in his Nobel Prize address (Malcolm Cowley, editor, *The Portable Faulkner* [rev. ed., New York, 1967]).

Index